OY, S.

914.676 ✓

D0785829

ESSENTIAL
COSTA BLANCA
AND ALICANTE

 Best places to see 34–55

Benidorm and the North 119–160

Original text by Sally Roy

Updated by Mona King

© Automobile Association Developments Limited 2009
First published 2007
Reprinted 2009. Information verified and updated

ISBN: 978-0-7495-6005-8

Published by AA Publishing, a trading name of Automobile Association Developments
Limited, whose registered office is Fanum House, Basing View, Basingstoke,
Hampshire RG21 4EA. Registered number 1878835.

A CIP catalogue record for this book is available from the British Library

A036 ... 008

Maps ...

About this book

This book is divided into five sections.

The essence of Costa Blanca and Alicante pages 6–19
Introduction; Features; Food and drink; Short break including the 10 Essentials

Planning pages 20–33
Before you go; Getting there; Getting around; Being there

Best places to see pages 34–55
The unmissable highlights of any visit to Costa Blanca and Alicante

Best things to do pages 56–79
Great places to have lunch; stunning views; top activities; souvenir ideas; places to take the children; best castles and more

Exploring pages 80–187
The best places to visit in Costa Blanca and Alicante, organized by area

Maps
All map references are to the maps on the covers. For example, Guadalest has the reference ✚ 21H – indicating the grid square in which it is to be found.

Admission prices
Inexpensive (under €4)
Moderate (€4–€8)
Expensive (over €8)

Hotel prices
Price are per room per night:
€ budget (under €35);
€€ moderate (€35–€70);
€€€ expensive to luxury (over €70)

Restaurant prices
Price for a three-course meal per person without drinks:
€ budget (under €6);
€€ moderate (€6–€15);
€€€ expensive (over €15)

Contents

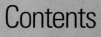

BEST THINGS TO DO

56 – 79

EXPLORING...

80 – 186

The essence of...

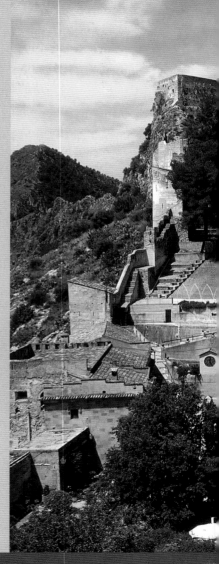

THE ESSENCE OF COSTA BLANCA

Holiday life on the Costa Blanca revolves around sun, sand and sea, with plenty of good food and a few late nights. If this is your first visit here, soak up the sun and the atmosphere, sparing perhaps a couple of days for exploring the beautiful inland mountains and one or two atmospheric towns. Once you have tasted the diversity of the region, you will probably return and gradually get to know the hidden corners, where traditional Spanish life has remained untouched by the glitz of the big resorts.

features

Most visitors to the Costa Blanca head for Benidorm, knowing that the Mediterranean's biggest resort will provide an unforgettable holiday. Many find everything they need in the coastal resorts – an agreeable year-round climate, a good standard of accommodation and plenty to do.

But the Costa Blanca has much more. Not far from the tourist centres traditional Spain re-emerges, a country where historic towns are set amid superb scenery and the rural pace of life remains undisturbed. Finding this other side is a challenge and delight, and the memory of this will last long after the tan has faded.

It is a land of huge variety, with thriving ports, bustling cities and a vast agricultural industry. Life has changed immensely in the last 50 years, but its people remain fiercely proud of their region, their history, their traditions and their culture. For most visitors though, the main attraction will be the beauty and fertility of the land. High sierras soar

above terraced valleys planted with almonds, oranges and olives. Discover the vineyards, hidden upland streams, and vistas of buff, red and ochre peaks. Explore the still lonely coastal stretches, where pines shade rocky paths and the air is scented with aromatic plants. Gaze over the salt flats, haunt of wading birds, a flat and shimmering landscape backed by miles of rich market gardens. The sooner you discover *this*

Costa Blanca, the more you'll enjoy this lovely corner of Europe.

GEOGRAPHY AND CLIMATE

- The Costa Blanca officially lies along the coastline of the region of Valencia, but this book includes the hinterland and the region of Murcia.
- At 325km (202 miles), the Segura is Spain's eighth longest river.
- Espuña, with a height of 1,585m (5,200ft) is the area's highest mountain.
- There is one regional park and several natural parks, including marine reserves, within the area.
- The northern part of the Costa Blanca enjoys 3,147 hours of sunshine annually, and the southern 3,098 hours.
- The annual rainfall ranges from 394 to 148mm (15.5 to 5.8in) and occurs mainly in the winter.

PEOPLE

- The population of the area is over 2,500,000, most living in the cities and their suburbs.
- Around only 50 per cent of the area's inhabitants were born here of local parents.
- More than 70 per cent of foreign property owners are English or German.

AGRICULTURE AND INDUSTRY

- The main fruit crops are oranges, lemons, cherries, peaches, nectarines and loquats.
- Large amounts of almonds and olives are grown here and are important Spanish exports.
- Local produce includes rice, tomatoes, peppers, courgettes, beans, aubergines and lettuces, which are exported throughout Europe.
- Fruit and nut processing are major industries.
- Shoe manufacture is an important source of revenue.

food & drink

The cooking of this part of Spain has a robust style all of its own, using the freshest seafood, locally raised meat and lots of fruit and vegetables; the classic *montaña y mar* combination of the coastal regions of Spain.

MAR Y TIERRA

Rice is the culinary king: *paella valenciana* springs to mind at once, but much more typical are dishes such as *arroz abanda* and *caldera* on the coast, *arroz con costra* and *paella huertanos* on the plains, and *arroces serranos* in the hills. These truly local dishes combine rice with tiny fish, with pork and vegetables, and with game and wild herbs. Traditionally only part of a meal, these are followed by fish dishes, robust stews or spit-roasted meat. Look out for *gazpacho de mero*, a fish stew served with flatbread, grilled *emperador* and *lenguado*, swordfish and sole, and large, whole fish baked in a salt crust – *dorada al sal*. Succulent *cochinillo*, suckling pig, the inland *gazpachos*, highly spiced meat stews eaten with flatbread, or *trigo picado*, a traditional cracked wheat dish, are all excellent. Winter country stews include *olleta* and *giraboix*, based on dried beans and meats cooked with mountain herbs and saffron. In Murcia the freshness of local produce spills over into the cooking: green garlic and sweet *pimentón* (paprika) flavour dishes inspired by the huge range of fruit and vegetables.

DESSERTS AND SWEETS

Local oranges, lemons, peaches, cherries and other fruit appear alongside the ubiquitous *flan* (caramel custard), and feature in tarts and as glacé fruits. Almonds are everywhere; popular in ultra-sweet Moorish-inspired biscuits, sumptuous puddings and cakes, often flavoured with local honey. Sampling *turrón* – an almond-based confection traditionally eaten at Christmas – is a must.

SNACKS

Main meals apart, there is still plenty to try. *Tapas*, the small platefuls of food served with drinks, can easily substitute for lunch or dinner. Fish, shellfish, olives, slices of ham and sausage, vegetable specialities and local almonds are just a few of the offerings in many bars. Just point and ask for a *porción* or a *ración*. Do as many natives do and have breakfast out – what could be more heavenly than *churros*, the long sugar-dusted doughnuts, dipped into a steaming cup of coffee or thick hot chocolate?

THIRST-QUENCHERS AND WINES

The Costa Blanca produces some excellent wines from the main areas of Monóvar (Monòver) and Jumilla – the red from the latter region with an astonishing 18 per cent alcohol content. Monóvar makes deep reds and delicate rosés as well as a famous dessert wine, Fondillón. The lesser-known Pinosa and Ricote wines are good and moscatel is the region's distinctive dessert wine. Alicante has its own herbal digestive, Cantueso. *Sangría*, *cava*, fresh orange juice, *horchata* – a nut-milk drink made from almonds or tiger nuts – and *granizada*, a fruit slush, all slip down well at different times of the day.

short break

If you have only a short time to visit Costa Blanca and would like to take home some unforgettable memories you can do something local and capture the flavour of the region. The following suggestions will give you a wide range of sights and experiences that won't take very long, won't cost very much and will make your visit very special. If you choose only one of these, you will have found something of the true heart of the region.

- **Bake in the sun** on a sandy beach or enjoy a swim off one of the rocky headlands on the northern coast. There

are some impressive pine-studded cliffs and solitary coves south of Cabo de la Nao (Cap de la Nau), stretches of dune-backed secluded sand between Alicante (Alacant) and Torrevieja, and remote, empty bays and beaches at Calblanque.

- **For lunch, fill up** on a selection of *tapas*, delicious bar snacks ranging from fresh seafood, *tortilla* and olives, to dried ham, crumbly *Manchego* cheese and salted almonds. *Tapas* bars abound all over Spain, and are an excellent way to feel the spirit of a place. Don't be put of by the dark interiors—these are often the best.

- **Take the scenic Costa Blanca Express** between Alicante (Alacant) and Dénia for great views and glimpses of small-town life; or hop on at night and have dinner up the coast from your resort.

● **Explore inland from the coast** and discover hilltop villages, lush market gardens, historic towns and splendid mountain landscapes. North of Benidorm the high sierras rise precipituously from the coast: wonderful mountain systems of great drama, the bare rockfaces glowing with different colours as the ligh changes throughout the day.

● **Pass an evening Spanish-style:** take a stroll along a palm-lined boulevard, have a leisurely drink, do a little late shopping, have dinner at 10:30 and listen to some live music. Many bars have music with jazz, easy listening and even the occasional burst of flamenco.

● **Indulge yourself with a gastronomic day out** sampling local wine, traditional paella and *turrón*, a delicious almond-based confection produced here and eaten at Christmas. The smaller the restaurant the higher the chance of finding real Spanish food; the buzz of Spanish voices will tell you if you're on the right track.

● **Take in a fiesta,** be it the pre-Lent *Carnaval*, the Holy Week processions, or a Moros y Cristianos parade commemorating the Reconquest. Forty-six provincial towns in Alicante (Alacant) hold Moros y Cristianos festivals; they take the form of often lavishly costumed historical re-enactments of key events during the years leading to the Moors' expulsion, with processions, fireworks, music and traditional food and drink.

● **Take a boat ride** for the fresh breezes and a change of scene, to the offshore island of Tabarca, Benidorm Island (a nature reserve), or the islands in the Mar Menor. There are plenty of entertaining boat excursions to be had up and down the Costa Blanca.

● **Tuck into a Benidorm English breakfast** complete with real tea and all the trimmings. If you don't join all the other holiday makers taking part in this Costa Blanca ritual you'll begin to wonder what you're missing out on.

● **Go to a local market** and admire the produce, smell the flowers and buy a picnic, a paella pan or a pair of locally made sandals. There are two distinct main types of market in Spain: the *mercado municipal*, a daily food market, and the *mercadillos*, weekly street markets.

Planning

Before you go

WHEN TO GO

JAN	FEB	MAR	APR	MAY	JUN	JUL	AUG	SEP	OCT	NOV	DEC
14°C	15°C	17°C	18°C	22°C	26°C	29°C	29°C	28°C	23°C	18°C	15°C
57°F	59°F	63°F	64°F	72°F	79°F	84°F	84°F	82°F	73°F	64°F	59°F

● High season   ● Low season

The Costa Blanca, and its main town Alicante, are favoured by a year-round sunny Mediterranean climate, with temperatures that make outdoor activities feasible in every season.

Winters are mild, with temperatures rarely falling below 10°C (50°F) during the day, even in midwinter, with some variations between the coastal and inland regions. The coldest months of the year are January, February and March. By February, however, spring has arrived, delightful when the almond blossom is out, while the end of March starts to attract the first batch of sunbathers to the beaches.

By the end of June temperatures are in the high 20s°C (low 80s°F) and can soar to over 34°C (93°F) during July and August, remaining high until November, when the area can be subject to rain and unsettled weather.

WHAT YOU NEED

	Required	Some countries require a passport to remain valid for a minimum period (usually at least six months) beyond the date of entry – contact their consulate or embassy or your travel agent for details.	UK	Germany	USA	Netherlands	Spain
●	Required						
○	Suggested						
▲	Not required						
Passport (or National Identity Card where applicable)			●	●	●	●	▲
Visa (regulations can change – check before you travel)			▲	▲	▲	▲	▲
Onward or Return Ticket			▲	▲	●	▲	▲
Health Inoculations (tetanus and polio)			▲	▲	▲	▲	▲
Health Documentation (➤ 23, Health insurance)			●	●	●	●	▲
Travel Insurance			○	○	○	○	○
Driving Licence (national)			●	●	●	●	●
Car Insurance Certificate			●	●	●	●	●
Car Registration Document			●	●	●	●	●

WEBSITES

Official tourist offices
www.costablanca.org
www.benidorm.org
www.denia.net
www.murciaturistica.es

www.marmenor.net
www.aytoorihuela.com
www.infoxativa.com
www.spain.info/uk
www.okspain.org/

TOURIST OFFICES AT HOME

In the UK

Spanish Tourist Office
✉ PO Box 4009,
London W1A 6NB
☎ 020 7486 8077
www.spain.info/uk

In the USA

Tourist Office of Spain
✉ 666 5th Avenue,
New York, NY 10103
☎ 212/265 8822
www.okspain.org/

HEALTH INSURANCE

Nationals of EU and certain other countries are entitled to receive free medical treatment in Spain with the relevant documentation (EHIC/ European Health Insurance Card), although private medical insurance is still advised and is essential for all other visitors.

Dental treatment is not usually available free of charge as all dentists practise privately. A list of *dentistas* can be found in the yellow pages of the telephone directory. Dental treatment should be covered by private medical insurance but visitors are advised to check their insurance cover before travelling.

TIME DIFFERENCES

| GMT 12 noon | Spain 1PM | Germany 1PM | USA (NY) 7AM | Netherlands 1PM | France 1PM |

Like the rest of Spain, the Costa Blanca is one hour ahead of Greenwich Mean Time (GMT+1), but from late March until late October summer time (GMT+2) operates.

NATIONAL HOLIDAYS

1 January *New Year's Day*
6 January *Epiphany*
March/April *Good Friday, Easter Monday*
1 May *Labour Day*
15 August *Assumption of the Virgin*
12 October *National Day*

1 November *All Saints' Day*
6 December *Constitution Day*
8 December *Immaculate Conception*
25 December *Christmas Day*

Many shops and offices close for longer periods around Christmas and Easter, as well as for the festivals of Corpus Christi in May/June and the local holiday of the comunidad valenciano on 9 October.

WHAT'S ON WHEN

January *Los Reyes Magos:* parades to celebrate the arrival of the Three Kings, in towns all over the Costa Blanca.
Porrate de San Antón (Fira i Porrat de Sant Antoni): a countryside festival with parades, decorated traditional horse-drawn carts, a food festival and a blessing of farm animals, Alicante, Benidorm.

February *Carnaval:* a pre-Lent carnival with parades and dancing in fancy dress, takes place in many towns.

March/April *Semana Santa:* week-long deeply religious Holy Week celebrations in towns everywhere and particularly noteworthy in Cartagena, Jumilla, Murcia, Moratalla, Mula, Orihuela, Alicante and Elche (Elx).
Peregrina de Santa Faz: 100,000-strong pilgrimage to the monastery at Santa Faz, Alicante.
Fiesta de la Primavera: parades and fireworks in the week following Holy Week; it includes the *Bando de la Huerta* (Orchard Procession) and the *Entierra de la Sardina* (Burial of the Sardine), Murcia.
Fallas de San José: fire-festival with effigies burned on pyres, Dénia.
Moros y Cristianos: the most important of the numerous festivals held to celebrate the Reconquest, Alcoy (Alcoi).

Semana Mediterránea de la Música: with top classical performers and orchestras from around the world, Alicante.

June *Hogueras de San Juan:* week-long midsummer festival with parades, fireworks and bullfights, Alicante. Smaller *hogueras* in Dénia, Calpe (Calp), Benidorm and Jávea (Xàbia).

July *Festival Español de la Canción:* major Spanish song festival, Benidorm.
Moros y Cristianos: spectacular historical mock-battle on beach, Villajoyosa (La Vila Joiosa).
Fiesta de la Virgen del Carmen: processions, boat races, fireworks, Villajoyosa, Tabarca, San Pedro.

August *Festival de las Habaneras:* festival of Cuban song-form brought back by salt-exporters, Torrevieja.
Misteri d'Elx, La Festa: superb medieval mystery play in two parts, celebrating the Assumption of the Virgin, Elche.
Moros y Cristianos: historical festival with the protagonists arriving from the sea, Dénia and Jávea.
Fiesta de la Vendimia: the town fountain runs with wine to celebrate the start of the wine harvest, Jumilla.
Festival Nacional del Canta de las Minas: one of the Spain's most important flamenco events, La Unión.

September *Festival de Folklore del Mediterráneo:* international festival with performances by groups from all over the world, Murcia.

October, November and December Small local festivals, listed under town entries.

Getting there

BY AIR

El Altet Airport

10km (6 miles) to city centre

🚈 N/A

🚌 30 minutes

🚕 20 minutes

Manises Airport

15km (9 miles) to city centre

🚈 10 minutes

🚌 40 minutes

🚕 20 minutes

Spain's national airline, Iberia (tel: 902 40 05 00 (in Spain); 0870 609 0500 (in the UK); www.iberia.com) has scheduled flights to Alicante's El Altet airport (10km/6 miles from Alicante's city centre) and Valencia's Manises airport (15km/9 miles from Valencia's city centre) from major Spanish and European cities.

Alicante's airport has only one terminal and there is a taxi rank directly outside the terminal building. The journey time is about 20 minutes to Alicante city centre and costs around €12–€15. A bus goes from outside the terminal every hour and the journey takes about 30 minutes to the centre of Alicante.

There are bus, taxi and metro connections to Valencia city centre from Manises airport. The metro has been operating only since 2007.

BY ROAD

Most visitors to the Costa Blanca travel by air to Alicante, with a high proportion opting for a package holiday. Car rental is readily available at reasonable prices at major centres.

For travellers wishing to drive down from the UK, there are car ferry services from Portsmouth to Santander and Plymouth to Santander (Brittany Ferries, tel: 0870 556 1600 in the UK; 942 36 06 11 in Spain; www.brittanyferries.com) and Portsmouth to Bilbao (P&O Ferries, tel: 08716 645 645; www.poferries.com), with excellent motorways down to the Costa Blanca. Alternative routes are by ferry to Calais, other ports in northern France or the Shuttle train service through the Channel Tunnel between Folkestone and Calais (journey time: 35 minutes; tel: 08705 35 35 35 in the UK; www.eurotunnel.com), a drive through France, entering Spain by its eastern border and the motorway south via Barcelona.

CUSTOMS
The allowances are:
from another EU country for personal use (guidelines)
800 cigarettes, 200 cigars, 1kg of tobacco
10 litres of spirits (over 22%)
20 litres of aperitifs
90 litres of wine, of which 60 litres can be sparkling wine
110 litres of beer
from a non-EU country for your personal use
200 cigarettes OR 50 cigars OR 250g of tobacco
1 litre of spirits (over 22%)
2 litres of intermediary products (such as sherry) and sparkling wine
2 litres of still wine
50g of perfume
0.25 litres of eau de toilette

The value limit for goods is €175

Travellers under 17 years of age are not entitled to the tobacco and alcohol allowances.

No drugs, firearms, ammunition, offensive weapons, obscene material, unlicensed animals are allowed.

Getting around

PUBLIC TRANSPORT

Trains The Costa Blanca is served by two railway systems: one links the main towns and runs to Madrid; the other is a narrow-gauge line which runs from Alicante to Dénia. The main RENFE (the Spanish railway network) lines link Cartagena, Alicante and Valencia, Alicante and Madrid, and Cartagena with Murcia (tel: 965 92 02 02, bookings – English language, tel: 902 24 02 02; www.renfe.es). The narrow-gauge railway line serving the Costa Blanca Express, run by FGV, is currently being electrified. From Alicante, departures are from the harbour or by the municipal market; the line now runs inland for part of the journey, with changes before reaching Benidorm and Dénia. For information on the changing situation, tel: 900 72 04 72. The Costa Blanca Express, run by FGV, leaves Alicante hourly from its own station and runs along the coast, stopping at virtually every station. Trains go as far as Benidorm, with about half completing the 2 hour 15 minute journey to Dénia (information and reservations: tel: 900 72 04 72).

Costa Blanca buses Alicante's bus station (tel: 965 13 07 00) is located on the Calle Portugal 17, from where buses leave for all over the province and further afield. There are several different companies serving the area; their buses run hourly along the coast and link the province's towns. Tickets, with numbered seats, are bought in advance, and tourist information offices can provide details. In Murcia buses run from the bus station on Calle Bolos s/n (tel: 968 29 22 11).

Boat trips Tabarca is the main island of the cluster lying off the coast to the south of Alicante; excursion ferries run from Alicante, Santa Pola and Torrevieja from April to November, giving a day on the island to explore and swim (information: Kon Tiki Alicante, tel: 965 21 63 96; Barco Santa Pola a Tabarca, tel: 965 41 11 13; Cruceros Tabardo, tel: 66 70 21 22).

Urban transport Local buses serve the main towns. Timetables and maps are available at local tourist information offices.

TAXIS

Hired at ranks (indicated by a blue square with a 'T'), on the street (by flagging down those with a green light/*libre* sign), or at hotels. They are good value, but may legally only carry four people. Check the approximate fare before setting out. A tariff list is displayed at taxi ranks.

DRIVING

- Driving is on the right.
- An international driving licence is required for North American visitors.
- The speed limit on motorways (*autopistas*) is 120kph (74mph); on main roads 100kph (62mph) and on minor roads 70–90kph (43–56mph).
- Seat belts must be worn in the front seats at all times and in rear seats where fitted.
- It is against the law to drive under the influence of drink; random breath testing is carried out.
- Fuel (*gasolina*) is generally available in three grades: Super Plus (98 octane), Super (96 octane), both unleaded, and *gasoleo* or *gasoil* (diesel). Petrol stations are normally open 6am–10pm, though larger ones (often self-service) are open 24 hours. Most take credit cards.
- If your car breaks down and you are a member of an AIT-affiliated motoring club, you can call the Real Automóvil Club de España (tel: 915 93 33 33). If the car is rented, follow the instructions in the documentation; most international rental firms provide a rescue service.

CAR RENTAL

The leading international car rental companies have offices at Alicante airport and in most of the main towns and resorts. You can book a car in advance (essential in peak periods) either direct or through a travel agent.

FARES AND CONCESSIONS

Holders of an International Student Identity Card can obtain some concessions, but package-holiday resorts are not really geared up for students, being more suited for families and senior citizens. Camping is excellent value and there are hostels and inexpensive hotels.

Older travellers will find good deals, especially in winter when the resorts are quieter and hotels offer very economical long-stay rates. The best deals are available through specialist senior citizens' tour operators.

Being there

TOURIST OFFICES

TOURIST INFORMATION TELEPHONE SERVICE
☎ 901 300 600

TOURIST INFORMATION OFFICES

Alicante (Alacant)
✉ Rambla Méndez Núñez 23.
Alicante 03002
☎ 965 20 00 00

Benidorm
✉ Avenida Martinez Alejoz 6,
Benidorm 03500
☎ 965 85 32 24

Dénia
✉ Plaza Oculista Buigues 9,
Dénia 03700
☎ 966 42 23 67

Elche (Elx)
✉ Plaza Parque 3, Elche 03203
☎ 966 65 81 96

Murcia
✉ Plaza del Romea 4
☎ 902 10 10 70

Orihuela ✉ Palacio Rubalcava,
Calle Francisco Diez 25, Orihuela
0330 ☎ 965 30 27 47

Other offices include: Altea, Águilas, Benissa, Calpe (Calp), Cartagena,
Gandía, Jávea (Xàbia), Mazarrón, Santa Pola, Torrevieja, Villajoyosa (La Vila
Joiosa) and Játiva (Xàtiva).

MONEY
Spain's currency is the euro (€), which is divided into 100 cents. Coins
come in denominations of 1, 2, 5, 10, 20 and 50 cents, €1 and €2, and
notes come in €5, €10, €20, €50, €100, €200 and €500 denominations.

TIPS AND GRATUITIES

Yes ✓ No ✗		
Restaurants (if service not included)	✓	5–10%
Cafés/bars	✓	change
Tour guides	✓	€1–€2
Taxis	✓	5%
Chambermaids/porters	✓	€1–€2
Toilets	✗	

POSTAL AND INTERNET SERVICES

Post offices *(correos)* are open 9am–2pm but some also open in the afternoon and on Saturday morning. The main post office in Alicante at Calle Alemania is open Monday to Friday 8:30–8:30, Saturday 9:30–1. Murcia's main office at Plaza de Ceballos is open Monday to Friday 9am–2pm, 5–8pm (till 2pm Saturday). Stamps may also be bought in *estancos* (tobacconists). Post boxes are yellow.

Certain hotels in the major centres offer internet services, either in the rooms or in the foyer, and there are internet cafés (cyber cafés) across the region, such as Cyber Internet Café, Calle de San Vicente 46, Alicante and Domino Bar, Carrer Martínez Oriola 15, Benidorm.

TELEPHONES

A public telephone *(teléfono)* takes all denomination euro coins. A phonecard *(credifone)* is available from *tabacos* and many supermarkets for €5 and €10.

The code for Alicante province is 965 and for Murcia 968. To call the international operator dial 1008 (in Europe) or 1005 (outside Europe). The number for directory enquiries is 11818 (national directory) and 025 (international directory).

International dialling codes
UK: 00 44
Germany: 00 49
USA and Canada: 00 1
Netherlands: 00 31

Emergency telephone numbers
The national number for all emergency services is **112** from any phone box.
Police (Policía Nacional) 091;
(Policía Local) 092
Fire (Bomberos) 080;
(Bomberos Local) 085
Ambulance (Ambulància) 061;
Alicante 965 14 40 00
Red Cross (Cruz Roja)
Alicante 965 25 25 25

EMBASSIES AND CONSULATES

UK ☎ 965 21 60 22
Germany ☎ 965 21 70 60

USA ☎ 963 51 69 73
Netherlands ☎ 965 21 21 75

HEALTH ADVICE

Sun advice The sunniest (and hottest) months are July and August with an average of 11 hours of sun a day and daytime temperatures of 32°C (90°F). You should avoid the midday sun and use a strong sunblock.

Drugs Prescription and non-prescription drugs and medicines are available from pharmacies *(farmacias)*, distinguished by a large green cross. Spanish pharmacists are highly trained and can dispense many drugs that would be available only on prescription in other countries.

Safe water Tap water is generally safe but can be heavily chlorinated. Mineral water is cheap to buy and is sold as *con gaz* (carbonated) and *sin gaz* (still). Drink plenty of water during hot weather.

Petty crime The national police force, the Policía Nacional keep law and order in urban areas. If you need a police station ask for *la comisaría*. To help prevent crime:

- Do not carry more cash than you need
- Do not leave valuables on the beach or poolside
- Beware of pickpockets in markets, tourist sights or crowded places
- Avoid walking alone in dark alleys at night

ELECTRICITY

The power supply is 220–225 volts. Sockets accept two-round-pin-style plugs. A transformer is needed for appliances operating on 110–120 volts.

OPENING HOURS

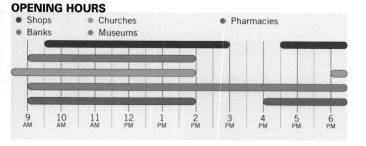

Large department stores, supermarkets and shops in tourist resorts may open outside these times, especially in summer. At least one pharmacy stays on duty in each town outside normal hours and at night.

LANGUAGE

The language that you hear on the streets in the towns and villages of Alicante is likely to be either Castilian (Spanish proper) or Valencian, a written and spoken language that is closely related to Catalan.

yes	*sí*	goodnight	*buenas noches*
no	*no*	excuse me	*perdóneme*
please	*por favor*	do you speak	*¿hablá ingles?*
thank you	*gracias*	English?	
welcome	*bienvenido*	how much?	*¿cuánto?*
hello	*hola*	open	*abierto*
goodbye	*adiós*	closed	*cerrado*
good morning	*buenos días*	today	*hoy*
good afternoon	*buenas tardes*	tomorrow	*mañana*
hotel	*hotel*	bath	*baño*
breakfast	*desayuno*	shower	*ducha*
double room	*habitación doble*	balcony	*balcón*
one person	*una persona*	key	*llave*
one night	*una noche*	lift	*ascensor*
reservation	*reservacíon*	sea view	*vista al mar*
bank	*banco*	travellers' cheque	*cheque de viajero*
money	*dinero*	credit card	*tarjeta de crédito*
cheque	*cheque*	change money	*cambiar dinero*
bank card	*tarjeta del banco*	foreign currency	*moneda extranjera*
breakfast	*desayuno*	beer	*cerveza*
lunch	*almuerzo*	wine	*vino*
dinner	*cena*	water	*agua*
bill	*cuenta*	coffee	*café*
aeroplane	*avión*	port	*puerto*
airport	*aeropuerto*	ticket	*billete*
train	*tren*	car	*coche*
bus	*autobús*	petrol	*gasolina*
boat	*barca*	where is...?	*¿dónde está....?*

Best places to see

1

Calblanque

www.marmenor.net

A remote and untouched stretch of coast, Calblanque has secluded bays and beaches, flowers, birds and solitude.

A few kilometres south of the highly developed resorts around the Mar Menor lies one of Spain's most unspoiled coastal stretches, Calblanque. Local people fought hard in the 1980s to protect this area, which is now a designated natural park.

Access is down a bumpy track off the busy main road running to La Manga. Within minutes, the roar of traffic disappears, hills rise up and the road gradually winds down to the sea. From the small car park boardwalks lead across the fragile dunes to the beaches, and paths run along the coast in either direction. If you are looking for an unspoiled beach,

this is it. The fine sands and crystal-clear water are only part of the experience, and it's worth leaving the beach to walk along the coast or explore the inland hills. A track runs south towards Cabo Negrete and the lighthouse at Punta Negra. Follow it down to see impressive rock formations caused by water erosion, lovely views and tempting swimming coves. The waters here are wonderfully clear and limpid, with protected underwater vegetation and sea creatures – perfect for keen scuba divers and snorkellers. A scramble in the hills behind the coast will give you an idea of the incredible richness of Calblanque's flora and fauna. Apart from other walkers, you may meet a herdsman and his goats.

Calblanque's main attraction is its peace, and its survival as an unspoiled enclave is a good example of what determined public opinion can achieve.

➕ 6A ✉ 70km (43 miles) east of Murcia 🍴 Bar occasionally open in summer (€) 🚌 Bus from Cartagena or La Unión to La Manga and 30- to 50-min walk
ℹ Small information office in park. Irregular opening hours
☎ 968 50 64 83 (Cartagena office)

2 Castillo de Santa Bárbara, Alicante

www.comunitatvalenciano.com

This should be the first stop on a tour of Alicante and is a perfect way to get your bearings, while admiring amazing views of the town and coastline.

The rambling complex of fortifications known as the Castillo de Santa Bárbara dominates Alicante (Alacant) from its position on the summit of Monte Benecantil. Rising dramatically on a bare rock above the town, the castle is best viewed from the oldest quarter of Alicante, the *villa vieja*, in the Barrio de Santa Cruz.

The site has certainly been fortified since prehistoric Iberian times and the Carthaginians,

Romans and Moors all built here from the 3rd century BC. No traces of their work remain and today's structures date mainly from the 16th century. The castle was repeatedly attacked but proved impregnable until the War of the Spanish Succession; assaulted from the sea in 1706 by Sir John Leake, it fell to Philip V's French troops in 1708, and was blown up by them in 1709, killing the English garrison. Undeterred, the English returned a century later and occupied the castle throughout the Peninsular War.

Today, the main attraction is the superb view from the top, a vast panorama over the town, from the palm-flanked Explanada through the 19th-century streets and shady plazas to the old quarter, and up and down the coast with its curving white beaches, headlands, port and marina. You can walk, drive up or take a lift from the Playa del Postiguet, which ascends through a shaft cut into the hill.

✠ *Alicante 7d* ✉ Above Playa del Postiguet, Alicante
☎ 965 16 21 28 or 965 26 31 31 ⏰ Apr–Sep daily 10–8;
Oct–Mar daily 9–7. Lift operates at same times ♿ Castle
free; lift moderate ❚❚ None on site 🚌 G, S
ℹ Alicante: Rambla Méndez Núñez 23 ☎ 965 20 00 00

3 Gallinera Valley

**One of the loveliest of valleys, the Vall de
Gallinera is best seen when the blossom of
the almond and cherry trees cloaks the
slopes in pink and white.**

The dramatic mountains behind the northern Costa
Blanca are cut by valleys, some narrow and steep,
others broad and gentle. They are all exceptionally
fertile, meticulously terraced where needed and
irrigated by a system devised by the Moors. These
valleys are nicknamed after the main crop: the
Gallinera has long been known as the Cherry Valley.

A twisting and scenic road runs inland from Pego
the whole way up to the village of Planes, passing
through superb landscapes. The land was first
settled and cultivated by the Moors and you can still
trace their influence in the names and layout of the
villages. The *Moriscos*, Christianized Moors, stayed
on here after the Reconquest and were only finally
expelled in 1609. The terracing on the hillside is
often Moorish, and walkers can find the ruins of

their dry-stone houses. The valley
is heavily planted with cherry
trees, iridescent green and white
in spring, speckled with crimson
fruit in summer, and interspersed
with orange, almond and olive
trees. Towering above are the
dramatic escarpments and peaks
of the sierras, with seductive little
roads twisting up the hillsides.

The main settlement is Planes,
a white, quintessentially Spanish
village, perched on a hill below a

ruined 12th-century castle, with a 16th-century aqueduct and a hidden blue swimming hole in the valley below.

The other tiny villages like Alcalá, Margarida, Benialfaquí and Benitaia all have their charms, their traditional way of life a perfect antidote to the more strident, upbeat attractions of the coastal resorts.

🕇 22J ✉ 50km (31 miles) north of Benidorm 🍴 Choice of restaurants and bars (€–€€€) 🚫 None ❓ Moros y Cristianos festival, Planes, 1st Sun in Oct. Most villages have their annual fiesta during Aug
ℹ From any of the northern resorts

4 Guadalest

www.guadalest.com

An excursion inland from Benidorm to this Moorish castle, encircled by mountains, makes an ideal early evening outing.

The mountains of the Sierra de Aitana rise steeply behind Benidorm's coastline, towering above lush and fertile valleys and dotted with hilltop villages. These valleys were terraced and irrigated by the Moors, who built a network of castles from which they controlled the northern valleys.

The most dramatically sited of these fortress villages is Guadalest, perched on a rocky crag above terraced orchards and a lake. Driving inland from the coast, the best view of its castle and bell tower, seemingly precariously balanced on the summit of a spectacular rock, is from the almond terraces and olive groves on either side of the twisting road. A few further bends and you reach the 15th-century Moorish castle, surrounded by a maze of narrow streets, whose only access is by a tunnel cut through the rock. Steep slopes drop to the reservoir below, and across the water the mountains, speckled with vegetation and cut by thread-like tracks, soar up over 1,066m (3,497ft).

Athough this castle was never overrun, Jaime I of Aragon took it after a lengthy siege in the 13th century. It successfully repelled Charles, Duke of Habsburg, during the War of the Spanish

Laid out in the 19th century, Huerto del Cura palms shelter stands of orange and pomegranate trees. Beside a lily pond deep in the garden stands a replica of the bust known as the Dama del Elx, a mysterious and enigmatic Iberian figure dating from 500BC and discovered in 1897 at the nearby hamlet of La Alcudia. The original is now in the Museo Arqueológico in Madrid.

The most famous tree is the Imperial Palm, a vast and ancient hermaphrodite with seven stems, six male and one date-bearing female, growing from one main trunk. The date crop from specific trees has traditionally been for consumption by famous Spaniards; two palms regularly supply King Juan Carlos and Queen Sofía with dates.

✚ 16H ✉ Porta de la Morera 49, Elche, 25km (15.5 miles) southwest of Alicante ☎ 965 45 19 36 🕐 Mar–Oct daily 9–7; Nov–Feb 9–6 🍴 Moderate 🍴 Bar (€) 🚻 E
ℹ Elche: Plaza del Parque 3 ☎ 966 65 81 96

6 Montgó and Cabo de San Antonio

www.xabia.org; **www.**denia.net

An unspoiled oasis of natural beauty, Montgó offers a chance to appreciate how this coastline and hinterland appeared before the tourist boom.

Easily reached from the holiday centres to the north and south, the massif of Montgó and the promontory of Planes run down to the Cabo de San Antonio (Cap de Sant Antoni) to the north of Jávea (Xàbia). This whole area, covering more than 2,000ha (4,940 acres), was designated a natural park in 1987, mainly because of its flora. Within the park more than 600 species of wild flowers grow, many of them unique indigenous sub-species. It is a sheer delight to wander the flower-bordered tracks and paths, breathing air scented with wild

rosemary and lavender and murmurous with bees. White, yellow, purple and pink predominate, the low-growing shrubs punctuated by miniature palms, heather, juniper, ilex and pines. The park has much bird life, with some rare gulls along the coast and birds of prey on higher ground.

For serious hikers, there is demanding walking up to the 753m (2,470ft) summit, with sweeping views up and down the coast, while the less energetic can enjoy several low-level routes. These mainly run through Planes, once heavily cultivated with raisin-vines and still scattered with smallholdings. A cypress-lined track takes you to Los Molinos, a line of old windmills above Jávea bay, last used in 1911. The walk (or drive) out to the lighthouse at the cape gives an opportunity for more lovely views and a chance to see the ruins of the tiny 14th-century hermitage dedicated to St Anthony, after whom the cape was named.

✚ 24G ✉ 40km (25 miles) north of Benidorm
☎ Information centre: 966 42 32 05 🍴 Choice of restaurants and bars in Jávea and Dénia (€–€€€)
🛈 Jávea: Plaza Almirante Bastarreche 11, Aduanas de Mar
☎ 965 79 07 36, and Plaza de la Iglesia 6 ☎ 965 79 43 56.
Dénia: Oculista Buigues 9 ☎ 966 42 23 67

7 Peñón de Ifach

www.calpe.es

**Peñón de Ifach (Penyal d'Ifac) is a
dramatic headland soaring over 300m
(985ft) up from the azure sea and
dominating the beaches on either side.**

No photograph can capture the impact of the huge
craggy outcrop, flanked by bustling family beaches,
that rears up from the sea at Calpe (Calp). This is
the Peñón de Ifach, the symbol of the Costa
Blanca, a looming mass of limestone, geologically
related to Gibraltar's rock and linked to the mainland
by a sandy isthmus. Legend claims Hercules first
charted the Peñón, and the remains of Roman
Calpea lie on its slopes. Ifach was certainly used as
a watchtower, with warning fires lit on the summit,
during the years when the Berber pirates
threatened the coast, and it was later renowned as
a smugglers' haven. Today, despite the teeming
summer crowds on Calpe's lovely beaches, it
remains isolated and untouched, thanks largely to
its modern role as a natural park.

A climb to the 332m (1,049ft) summit is best
tackled in the cool of the morning in the summer;
the views along the coastline and inland to the
sierras are at their best around sunrise. Allow about
an hour to reach the top, along the track which runs
through a tunnel in the bottom of the rock face. The
gentler lower slopes run down to rocky inlets and
tiny bays, and are brilliantly carpeted in spring with
a profusion of more than 300 species of wild
flowers and plants, including an orchid unique to
the Peñón. Bird life is prolific here; in winter the

rare Audouin's gull is a frequent visitor and flamingos inhabit the nearby salt flats, along with a variety of waders.

✚ 22G ✉ Calpe, 20km (12.5 miles) northeast of Benidorm ▮▮ Bars and restaurants in Calpe (€–€€€) ⛴ Ifach Charter ☎ 965 10 25 91 summer only ℹ Calpe: Avenida de los Ejércitos Españoles 44 ☎ 965 83 69 20 and Plaza del Mosquit s/n ☎ 965 83 85 32

8 San Feliu, Játiva (Xàtiva)

The evocative and beautiful 13th-century church of San Feliu is in a lovely position on wooded slopes overlooking the historic town of Játiva.

One of the region's finest religious buildings, lovely and evocative San Feliu (Sant Feliu) is set among olives and cypresses below the walls of Játiva's historic castle. A must for fans of early architecture, this ancient church stands on the site of a 7th-century palaeo-Christian church, the seat of the Visigothic bishopric.

The present building, one of the oldest in Valencia, was erected in 1269 on the orders of Jaime I, soon after his expulsion of the Moors. It has a single nave, split by four massive arches, and architecturally is surprisingly similar to Syrian churches of the same date. Only rarely used now for services, the church's walls are hung with superb Spanish Renaissance religious paintings, mainly from nearby churches and monasteries. Some are sadly in need of restoration, but the colours and gilding still glow.

The altarpiece was commissioned at the end of the 15th century and shows scenes from the life of Christ and the Virgin, flanked by images of Saints Cosmas and Damian, two early saints, and Saint Blaise, the patron saint of sore throats. The holy water stoup is carved with scenes from the Nativity, including a shepherd leading two rather charming pig-like sheep.

Along the external entrance walls runs a fine loggia. The roof of the loggia is supported by six Roman columns.

✠ 22M ✉ Carretera Castillo, Játiva, 60km (37 miles) north of Alicante 🕐 Apr–Sep Tue–Sat 10–1, 4–7, Sun 10–1; Oct–Mar Tue–Sat 10–1, 3–6, Sun 10–1 ✋ Free
🍴 Choice of restaurants and bars nearby (€–€€€)
🚌 Tourist train from outside the tourist office Mon–Sat 12:30, 4:30, Sun 12, 1, 4:30 🚋 From Alicante via Alcoy (Alcoi)
ℹ Alameda de Jaume I, 50 ☎ 962 27 33 46

Santa María, Murcia

www.murciaturistica.es

The façade of this lovely Mediterranean Gothic cathedral is the finest among Murcia's many examples of baroque architecture.

Murcia's cathedral, dating from the 14th to 18th centuries, stands out in a city crammed with exuberant baroque architecture. If ever a building captured the spirit of the place, Santa María, with its ebullient and lavish decoration and sense of religious fervour, surely does.

The cathedral's south side retains its Gothic façade, but the main west front was rebuilt after a flood in 1735. Designed by Jaime Bort, this feast of curves and swooping detail, only slightly restrained by its soaring Corinthian columns, is liberally dotted with statues of gesticulating saints, their robes tossed by some celestial wind.

The interior, retaining signs of its Gothic origin, is an extravagant example of florid plateresque. The high point is the Capilla de los Vélez, completed in 1507 and designed as a funeral chapel for a powerful local family. With its lovely screen and rich vaulting this must be one of

Spain's finest examples of Hispano-Gothic architecture. Other highlights include an urn containing the heart of 13th-century Alfonso the Wise in the Capilla Mayor and a 600kg (1,323-pound) gold and silver processional monstrance in the cathedral's museum. The choir contains a *Christ* by Murcia's famous 18th-century resident, Francisco Salzillo. He specialized in realistic polychrome wooden figures to be used in Holy Week processions; his work can be seen at the Museo Salzillo (➤ 164–165). A ramp and stairway lead up the 98m (321ft) 18th-century tower, which has great views.

🚩 *Murcia 4b* ✉ Plaza Hernández Amores 2 ☎ 968 21 63 44 ⏱ Daily 10–1, 5–7 💷 Cathedral free; museum moderate 🍴 Choice of bars and restaurants nearby (€–€€€) 🚌 26, 28, 39, 49
ℹ Plaza Cardenal Belluga s/n ☎ 968 35 87 49

10 Sierra de Espuña

www.sierraespuna.com

The contrast between the rocky peaks and pine forests of this high sierra and the coast below makes a day in this park an enjoyable change.

Southwest of Murcia city, the Andalucian sierras tail off into a series of rocky massifs, undeveloped and undiscovered. This is the Sierra de Espuña, one of Spain's renowned natural parks, a wilderness area of dramatic peaks and pine forests offering scenic drives, serious climbing and superb walking.

The forest was the inspiration of Ricardo Codorniú, an engineer charged in 1891 with finding a solution to the frequent and destructive floods which swept down from the sierra to the villages below. Huge areas of hillside were planted with Canary pine, cypresses and cedars, which stabilized the slopes and created this unique habitat. Over the last century more than 250 plant species have established themselves, and the forest is the home of wild boar, deer, mountain cats and tortoises, as well as more common woodland creatures. At 1,579m (5,180ft), the ochre peak of Espuña dominates the whole park area, frequently glimpsed through the trees from the road which runs through the park from Alhama to Aledo. This narrow, steep and tortuous road is one of Murcia's most beautiful, and gives access to different areas of Espuña. Waymarked walking trails run through the woods, tracks give access to challenging rock-climbs, and there are shady glades with natural springs and well laid-out picnic areas.

✚ 4F ✉ 25km (15.5 miles) south of Murcia ⊗ Always
open ⑪ Summer-only bar in park, restaurants and bars at
Alhama and Aledo (€–€€€) 🚌 From Murcia to Alhama
ⓘ Information in summer from the Casa Forestal de Huerta
Espuña inside the park. Murcia: Plaza Cardenal Belluga s/n
☎ 968 35 87 49

Best things to do

Great places to have lunch

Altamar (€€)

Standing right on the beach, this restaurant has a good bar and terrace and a great range of rice dishes.

✉ Jaime I 96, Playa de Muchavista, El Campello ☎ 965 65 66 33

Ca L'Angeles (€€)

Good country cooking, with many traditional dishes, served in a pleasantly converted old building.

✉ Gabriel Miró 12, Polop ☎ 965 87 02 26

El Cantó (€)

This is one of Alicante's best bets for a quick and delicious lunch. El Cantó is always packed with Spaniards.

✉ Calle de Alemania 26, Alicante ☎ 965 92 56 50

Casa Enrique (€)

A friendly local place with a bar and restaurant that offers excellent *arroz con costra*.

✉ Empedra 10, Elche ☎ 965 45 15 77

El Churra (€)

A pretty hotel restaurant serving classic Murcian recipes, offering a wide range of local vegetable specialities, plus excellent grilled steaks and a comprehensive wine list.

✉ Avenida Marqués de los Vélez 12, Murcia ☎ 968 23 84 00

L'Obrer (€€)

Popular tourist restaurant with a terrace serving traditional mountain dishes and grilled meat.

✉ Carretera de Benimantell 27, Guadalest ☎ 965 88 50 88

El Pegolí (€€)

Just outside town, this restaurant specializes in seafood and shellfish of all kinds.

✉ Fenix 13, Les Rotes, Dénia ☎ 965 78 10 35

El Rincón de las Jarres (€€)

Seafood and country dishes are the specialities in this lively bar-cum-restaurant.

✉ María Parodi 3, Torrevieja ☎ 965 71 09 60

Rosa (€)

This restaurant offers basic dishes and *tapas* with outside seating on an attractive little square shaded by palm trees.

✉ Plaza Santa Faz 2, Alicante ☎ 630 14 67 21

Sant Pere 24 (€€)

Wonderful rice and seafood dishes are served at this relaxed place down by the beach. Popular with locals.

✉ Playa de l'Olla, Calle San Pedro 24, Altea ☎ 965 84 49 72

Stunning views

Jávea (Xàbia) and its bay from the Cabo de San Antonio (Cap de Sant Antoni; ➤ 143).

South down the coast from Cabo de la Nao (Cap de la Nau; ➤ 134).

The Guadalest valley from the terrace below the Castillo de Guadalest (➤ 142).

The view to the hills and coast from the Coll de Rates (➤ 137).

The Peñón de Ifach (➤ 48–49) from above Calpe (Calp).

Alicante and the coast from the Castillo de Santa Bárbara (➤ 38–39).

The Sierra de Espuña from the pine woods of the natural park (➤ 54–55).

Benidorm's superb beaches from the Castillo-Mirador (➤ 121).

The Gallinera valley (➤ 40–41) from the Planes road.

Castillo de Játiva from below, and the views from the Castillo to the town (➤ 127).

Top activities

Cycling: Rent a bicycle to get around your resort and further afield. Side roads around the Mar Menor in the south or along the coast north of Benidorm are ideal for cyclists.

Golf: The Costa Blanca area has more than 20 prestigious and beautifully laid-out golf courses, as well as some smaller ones. Golf package holidays are increasingly popular. Most courses have clubs and trolleys or buggies for hire and a full range of services. You may be asked for a handicap certificate and you should book in advance.

Horse-riding: Experience the peace of the countryside on horseback.

Sailing: If you haven't tried it before, now's your chance. Inexperienced mariners will find sailing schools up and down the coast at all the main resorts with rental and tuition available, the sheltered Mar Menor being a particularly good spot for beginners.

Scuba diving: There are several stretches of protected coastline along the Costa Blanca with a rich underwater marine life. You can dive under supervision with the many diving clubs; if you want to dive alone bring your international proficiency certificate.

Swimming: Beaches vary on the coast, but often sport the Blue Flag, which guarantees cleanliness, safety and facilities. The main towns – Alicante, Benidorm and Murcia – have covered heated indoor pools for winter swimming, and most resort hotels have pools.

Tennis: There are clubs at all the resorts and many hotels have their own courts.

Walking: Mountain walking in the sierras is popular. Remember to let someone know where you are going and when you expect to be back, wear suitable clothes and footwear, be prepared for changes in weather, and take plenty of water and something to eat. Detailed maps are available from the Centro Nacional de Informacíon Geográfica, General Ibáñez de Ibero 3, 28003 Madrid (tel: 915 97 95 14; www.cnig.es). Local tourist boards will put you in touch with the relevant local groups.

Windsurfing: With its mild winter and long hot summers, the coast provides ideal conditions for windsurfing. Tuition and rentals are available through hotels and clubs; the Mar Menor is a good place to try if you're a novice.

a drive

around Guadalest and the Sierra de Aitana

Take the E15 motorway north from Alicante and take exit 65 on to the C3318 (70) running inland to Callosa de Ensarriá. Continue on this road to visit the Fuentes del Algar (▶ 139). Cut back to Callosa and take the C3313 (755) into the hills.

As the road climbs, terraces first levelled in Moorish times and washed with the pink of almond blossom in February cling to the lower slopes. The road rises steadily until a sharp corner brings Guadalest (▶ 42–43) into view.

After visiting the village and its castle, continue upwards past the white villages of Benimantell and Confrides to cross the pass of Puerto de Ares.

As you lose height, the vegetation changes and pines and olives dot the terraces and hillside.

Through Ares village turn left on to the A170 and past Alcolecha.

The country here in the superb landscape of the Sierra de Aitana is much wilder, scattered with pines, juniper and a plethora of wild herbs and aromatic shrubs.

After 9km (5.5 miles) take the left fork on to the A173 to Sella, passing the Safari Aitana wildlife park (▶ 71).

The upland scenery, with the peak of Aitana (1,558m/ 5,112ft) surging up from the valley, gives way gradually to impeccably kept terracing once more, orange and almond trees are underplanted with vegetables and salad plants.

Drive through Sella and after 6km (4 miles) take a left turn on to the A1741 to Finestrat, and then the A1735 to return to Benidorm, Alicante and the coast.

Distance 122km (76 miles)
Time 3 hours without stops or most of a day with visits
Start/end point Alicante 🚆 18H
Lunch La Fonda ✉ Carretera Alcoy 15, Sella ☎ 965 87 90 11

Souvenir ideas

Almonds – plain, roast or salted, are top quality and grown in the hills of the region. Toasted almonds are popular with drinks. Everything from soup to trout can be made *almendrada* – made from or cooked with almonds (➤ 13).

Belén figures – the intricate and delicate traditional figures used in Christmas Nativity cribs. Belén means Bethlehem, relating to the birthplace of Jesus.

Cane and basketware from the old town of Gata de Gorgos (➤ 140–141); baskets, trays, esparto (reeds) mats and furniture.

Ceramics and pottery, from cheerful hand-painted bowls and plates to a delicate Lladro figure. Tiles, glazed pottery and attractively painted crockery make excellent gifts or souvenirs.

Cotton goods – Spanish cotton is excellent quality. The most common items are tablecloths, placemats, napkins, bed linen and handkerchiefs.

Local wines and liqueurs – to remind you of visits to vineyards and atmospheric *bodegas* (► 15).

Paella pans – the best place to buy the real thing is a local street market.

Shoes and bags – locally produced soft leather footwear and elegant bags make an excellent buy.

Strings of dried garlic and peppers to brighten your kitchen and pep up your cooking.

Turrón – almost all of the traditional Christmas nougat is produced in the Costa Blanca, particularly in the town of Jijona (Xixona; ► 99). Alicante *turrón* is white and hard, and studded with whole nuts.

Best churches and convents

Numerous mosques were built by the Moors during their occupation of the region from the late 8th century. After the Reconquest in the mid-1200s, many mosques were turned into churches; particularly fine examples of baroque architecture can be seen in Orihuela and Murcia.

Catedral de San Salvador, Orihuela (➤ 91)

Colegio de Santo Domingo, Orihuela (➤ 93)

Concatedral de San Nicolás de Bari, Alicante (➤ 86)

Convento de Santa Clara, Murcia (➤ 164)

Ermita de San Feliu, Játiva (Xàtiva) (➤ 50–51)

Iglesia de San Bartolomé, Jávea (Xàbia) (➤ 143)

Iglesia de San Miguel, Murcia (➤ 164)

Iglesia de Santa Ana, Murcia (➤ 164)

Iglesia de Santa María, Alicante (➤ 86–87)

Santa María, Murcia (➤ 52–53)

Places to take the children

Aqualandia

The biggest, best-known and most popular aquapark in Benidorm.
A wide selection of rides, giant slides, swimming pools and
watersports, with bars and restaurants. ✉ Sierra Helada, Partida Bayo, Benidorm ☎ 965 86 40 06 ⑥ May to
mid-Oct daily 11–7 🚌 2, 7

Aquapolis

A big aquapark with pools, hydrotubs and plenty of slides and rides
for the children, with water mountains and artificial waves. Nicely
laid out with restaurants and a picnic area. ✉ Finca de la Hoya Grande s/n, Torrevieja ☎ 965 71 58 90 ⑥ Mid-Jun to
mid-Sep daily 11–7

Costa Blanca Express

All children will enjoy a ride on this scenic narrow-gauge train
which ambles up the coast from Alicante to Dénia, stopping en
route. Have a swim and some lunch and come home later in
the day. ✉ Alicante ☎ 900 72 04 72, Benidorm ☎ 965 85 18 95, and Dénia ☎ 965
78 04 45 ⑥ Daily 6am–9pm

Karting la Cala

A chance for older children to test their skill and nerves on one of
Europe's largest go-karting tracks. ✉ Carretera Benidorm–Villajoyosa, Km 143, Benidorm ☎ 965 89 46 76
⑥ Summer daily 10am–1am; winter daily 11–7

Mundomar

A marine park beside Aqualandia with a dolphin show; seals and
parrots are popular, too and there's a maze of wooded, rocky paths
and water features to explore. ✉ Sierra Helada, Rincón de Loix, Benidorm ☎ 965 86 91 01 ⑥ Daily 10–6
🚌 2, 7

Safari Aitana

A safari park in the Aitana Sierra behind the coast with the usual collections of lions, giraffes, elephants and other animals. It's a good choice in hot weather, when you can have a swim in the pool.

✉ Carretera Villajoyosa–Alcoy, Km 20 ☎ 965 52 92 73 🕓 Daily 11–6:30

Safari Park Vergel

A drive-round safari park near the beaches. There is also an opportunity to see a dolphin show.

✉ Carretera Vergel–Pego ☎ 965 75 02 85 🕓 Daily 10–5:45

Terra Mítica

A spectacularly large, 'World of Myth' theme park near Benidorm. Enjoy rides, shows and theatre events in five areas based on past Mediterranean civilizations – Egypt, Greece, Rome, Iberia and the Islands. Rides include a log flume and the largest wooden rollercoaster in Europe (the second largest in the world).

✉ Carretera Benidorm a Finestrat, Camino del Moralet s/n ☎ 965 00 43 00; www.terramiticapark.com 🕓 Summer daily 10am–midnight; mid-Sep to Oct, daily 10–8; winter daily 10–6

Terra Natura

New generation wildlife park where visitors can be in close contact with the animals. The park is divided into four themed areas: Pangea, America, Asia and Europe.

✉ Foia del Verdader, Benidorm ☎ 902 52 23 33; www.terranatura.com 🕓 Summer daily 10–midnight; winter daily 10–8

Top beaches

La Barraca, Cabo de la Nao
A beautiful bay, reached down a twisting road, and sheltered by high cliffs and the island of El Descubridor. Excellent swimming off the pebbly beach. Reasonable facilities generally available.

Cala Sardinera, Cabo de San Martín (Cap de Sant Martí)
Unspoiled rocky cove with pebbly beach sheltered by cliffs on the north side of Cabo San Martín. A hike through rocks and scrub from nearest parking, followed by a scramble down. No facilities.

Calblanque
Best places to see, ➤ 36–37.

La Granadella, Cabo del la Nao
Reached by road through pine woods. There's a bay sheltered by pine-covered cliffs. Crowded in summer. Reasonable facilities.

Guardamar del Segura
Guardamar's beach is backed by a unique system of sand dunes, planted with natural pine, eucalyptus and dune-grass, running down to a long beach. Spend the day in the sun or the cool shade of the pines. Good facilities.

Playa de Bolnuevo, Puerto de Mazarrón

Large area with variety of beaches and facilities. Bolnuevo proper has wonderful sand, sheltered by sandbars; opposite here wind and water have eroded the rocks into fantastic shapes. Hidden coves lie to the south with superb clear water, ideal for snorkelling and scuba diving. Good facilities.

Playa del Pedrucho, La Manga

The long strip of land separating the Mar Menor from the Mediterranean is seldom more than a kilometre (half a mile) across. The warm shallow water beaches on the inner side are ideal for small children, while the windier Mediterranean water shelves more steeply. The facilities are excellent.

Playa del Postiguet, Alicante

This Blue Flag beach in the city centre has excellent facilities and clear water, and the marina is an attractive leisure centre.

Playa de Venecia, Gandía

Huge stretch of white-sand beach with a reputation as one of the liveliest night-time beach areas. Gandía is renowned for its water sports, particularly sailing and windsurfing. Excellent facilities.

Museums

MARQ (Museo Arqueológico)
If you thought archaeology was dull, the state-of-the-art visual, light and sound effects at MARQ may help you change your mind (► 87).

Museo l'Almodi
Játiva's town museum housed in a fine Renaissance building (► 128).

Museo de Bellas Artes
A large and variable collection of pictures giving a comprehensive view of the development of Murcian painting from the 15th to the 20th centuries (► 164).
✉ Obispo Frutos 12, Murcia ☎ 968 23 93 46 🕐 Mon–Fri 9–2, 5–8, Sat 10–2 ✋ Moderate

Museo de la Catedral
In the cloister of Murcia's cathedral (► 52–53, 164), this museum houses early sculpture, and gives pride of place to the huge gold and silver monstrance, used at the feast of Corpus Christi.
✉ Plaza de la Cruz 2 ☎ 968 21 63 44 🕐 Apr–Sep daily 10–1, 5–8; Oct–Mar daily 10–1, 5–7 ✋ Inexpensive

Museo de la Ciencia
A science museum, with water as its main theme. Hands-on exhibits and a children's planetarium.
✉ Plaza de la Ciencia 1, Murcia ☎ 968 21 19 98 🕐 Tue–Sat 10–2, 5–8, Sun 11–2 🚌 7a

Museo del Juguete Antiguo 1790–1959

A toy museum (part of a complex of three museums) with a huge collection from all over the world; adults will get nostalgic over the comic collection and there's a reproduction of a 1929 schoolroom.

✉ Calle de la Virgen, Guadalest ☎ 965 88 53 23 ⏰ Jun–Sep daily 10–9; Oct–May daily 10–6 🚌 From Benidorm

Museo Municipal de la Festa

Come here for a taste of Elche's most important festival, the medieval mystery play devoted to the Virgin (➤ 96). State-of-the-art exhibits and a multimedia show give a real idea of the drama.

✉ Calle Mayor de la Vila 25, Elche ☎ 965 45 34 64 ⏰ Tue–Sat 10–1, 4:30–8:30, Sun 10–1

Museo Nacional de Arqueología Marítima

A collection of treasures from the sea-bed. Exhibits at this Cartagena museum include a reconstruction of a perfectly loaded ship (➤ 171).

Museo del Palmeral

If Elche's World Heritage Site Palm Forest (➤ 95–97) catches your imagination, this museum will fill you in on its history and importance, and you can hire a bicycle to explore the forest.

✉ Carrer Porta de la Morera 12, Elche ☎ 965 42 22 40 ⏰ Tue–Sat 10–1:30, 4:30–8, Sun 10:30–1:30

Museo Salzillo

A huge collection of work by the 18th-century wood sculptor Francisco Salzillo (➤ 164–165), who specialized in dramatic and detailed polychrome figures and scenes from the life of Christ. Most of these were designed to be carried through the streets during the Holy Week processions.

✉ Plaza San Agustín 3, Murcia ☎ 968 29 18 93 ⏰ Tue–Sat 10–2, 5–8, Sun 11–2 ✋ Moderate

Tapas

L'Albufera (€)
This popular restaurant is busy all day, thanks to the great range of *tapas*, good-value *menús* and splendid rice dishes.

✉ Calle Gerona s/n, Benidorm ☎ 965 86 56 61 🕐 Lunch and dinner

El Bocaito (€€)
Atmospheric and lively bar and restaurant, serving *tapas* and a good range of dishes with the emphasis on rice and shellfish.

✉ Isabel la Católica 22, Alicante ☎ 965 92 26 30 🕐 Lunch and dinner. Closed Mon

Cabo la Nau (€€)
Beautifully situated restaurant with terrace, perched on a high headland with splendid views. Good *tapas*, rice and fish.

✉ Faro Cabo de la Nau, Jávea ☎ 965 77 18 35 🕒 Lunch and dinner.
Closed Wed

Mesón el Corral (€€)
Right in the heart of the old town and decorated with hand-painted
azulejos, this friendly restaurant offers an enormous range of *tapas*
as well as a full menu.
✉ Plaza Santo Domingo 16, Murcia ☎ 968 21 45 97 or 968 21 49 85
🕒 Lunch and dinner

Piripi (€€)
Rice cooked to perfection is the speciality in this friendly family-run
restaurant with a huge range of *tapas* to start.
✉ Oscar Esplá 30, Alicante ☎ 965 22 79 40 🕒 Lunch and dinner

Tapas del Mundo (€)
Small family-run restaurant in the old town. Go along with the
proprietor's suggestions. The *tapas* served up here are creative
and delicious, in addition to carefully selected local wines. Very
friendly and welcoming service.
✉ Calle San Miguel 4, Benidorm ☎ 627 53 92 18 🕒 Lunch and dinner.
Closed Sun dinner

Tasca Eulalia (€€)
Long-established restaurant, known for the quality of its *tapas*.
Lively ambience; frequented by the locals.
✉ Marques de Campo 39, Dénia ☎ 965 78 64 79 🕒 Lunch and dinner

ZM 101 (€–€€€)
You can eat with your toes in the sand at this beachfront bar/
restaurant. It's great for lunch, a snack, dinner or just a drink, and
serves up a range of *tapas*, as well as fresh fish and grills.
✉ El Vivero, Playa de los Alemanes, La Manga, Murcia ☎ 968 33 72 84
🕒 Breakfast, lunch and dinner daily

Best castles

Between the 8th and 13th centuries many castles were built by the Moors for protection against outside threats. These ranged from tax collectors and neighbouring feudal lords to foreign invaders and pirates. There are nearly 100 castles left in the Costa Blanca area today.

Exploring

Since Spanish decentralization and the establishment of the autonomous regions in the 1980s, the Costa Blanca ('White Coast') strictly speaking is now only the area within the region of Valencia. The Murcian coast, running from San Pedro del Pinatar to Aguilas, is officially divided into the Costa Cálida in the north and the Costa del Almería in the south. As in so many parts of Spain, tourism here clings to the highly developed coastal strip, leaving the hinterland virtually untouched. Less than 15km (10 miles) inland from even the busiest resort, rural life continues as it has always done. Even beside the sea there are still solitary coves, stretches of dune-backed fine white sands and remote, empty bays where you can have a swim, rock scramble or a clifftop walk far from the sights and sounds of the 21st century. So if you crave tranquillity you will never have far to go from the Costa Blanca's modern hotels to find it.

Alicante and around

Alicante (Alacant), the provincial capital, is the Costa Blanca's main centre, a prosperous and bustling city in a fine coastal position, with interesting buildings, churches and museums, excellent restaurants, good shops and plenty of amenities and tourist facilities.

◻ Alicante

For anyone on holiday in the region, Alicante is a must – a good contrast to days on the beach. Within easy reach are the historic cities of Elche (Elx) and Orihuela, both fascinating in their own way, the wine-growing area around Monóvar (Monòver), and a string of Moorish castles and small white towns.

The scenery of the hinterland ranges from the mountains above the Vinalopó valley to the fertile plains, palm forests and salt flats behind the southern coast. Each of the seaside towns has its own character and charm, offering the essential holiday ingredients of sun, sand and sea.

ALICANTE (ALACANT)

Alicante has everything you would expect of a Mediterranean city: a long and honourable history, venerable buildings, palm-lined avenues and seafront *paseos*, and all the amenities of a thriving modern provincial centre. The first settlement was established by the Greeks, who founded a colony they called Akra Leuka, the 'white headland', near modern Alicante. The Romans followed, founding their city of Lucentum, the City of Light.

Like the rest of southern Spain, Alicante was invaded and settled by the Moors from the second half of the 8th century. For 500 years it was an Arab city and it was only in 1246 that Alfonso X regained it for the Castilian crown. In 1308 Alicante was incorporated into the kingdom of Valencia by Jaime III.

www.comunitatvalenciana.com

➕ 18H

🔢 Hogueras de San Juan (20–29 Jun); for additional festivals ➤ 24, or phone the tourist office

ℹ Rambla Méndez Núñez 23 ☎ 965 20 00 00

Ayuntamiento

The twin-towered 18th-century town hall is one of Alicante's finest baroque buildings. An ornate doorway in the centre of the façade opens into a vast hall, where a striking gold-plated sculpture of John the Baptist by Salvador Dalí stands by an elegant stairway which sweeps up to the state rooms and chapel on the first floor. Upstairs, the Salón Azul contains the city's earliest charter of privileges, and a small picture gallery. The lovely chapel is adorned with beautiful painted tiles, and over the altar hangs a painting of St Nicolás of Bari, the city's patron.

➕ *Alicante 6b* ✉ Plaza del Ayuntamiento 1 ☎ 965 14 91 00 🕒 Mon–Fri 8–1 🚌 G, H, M ✋ Free

Castillo de Santa Bárbara

Best places to see, ➤ 38–39.

The Centre

Alicante's centre consists of the old *barrios* (districts) clustered at the foot of Monte Benecantil, and the broad avenues of the 19th-century city. Head for the Santa Cruz district (➤ 88), to find some of the city's oldest buildings, 19th-century sanctuaries – and some great *tapas* bars. Ramblas Méndez Núñez demarcates the 19th-century commercial centre, home to the Mercado Central, one of the region's largest daily markets. The shopping area runs along the Avenida de Maisonnave and the streets around Avenida de Francisco Soto. This leads down to the 19th-century palm-shaded

Paseo Explanada de España, parallel to the sea. Behind this lie the port and marina, with bars and cafés.

✚ *Alicante 5b* 🍴 Choice of restaurants and bars (€–€€€) 🚌 F, G, H, K, L, M

Concatedral de San Nicolás de Bari

In the heart of the oldest part of the city stands the cathedral, built in the 17th century to replace the 13th-century church that stood on the site of the city's mosque. The façade is simple Renaissance in style, but the interior, with its soaring dome, is much closer to baroque, heavy with carving and gilt. The 15th-century cloister, reached through a side door, provides an effective contrast.

✚ *Alicante 6b* ✉ Plaza del Abad Canónigo Renalba s/n ☎ 965 21 26 62
🕐 Daily 6–7:30pm (and during Mass) ✋ Free 🍴 Restaurants/bars (€–€€€)
🚌 G, H, M

Iglesia de Santa María

Alicante's oldest church was built in the 14th century on the site of a mosque in the heart of the original Arab town. It has been frequently altered and is today a marvellous *mélange* of different

architectural styles. The baroque doorway leads into a nave, which is an outstanding example of Valencian Gothic. The great golden altar dates from the late 1400s and the font dates from the following century.

➕ *Alicante 7c* ✉ Plaza de Santa María ☎ 965 21 60 26 🕒 Daily 10:30–1, 6–7:30 ✋ Free 🍴 Choice of restaurants and bars nearby 🚌 G, H, M, P, S

MARQ (Museo Arqueológico)

Housed in a former hospital, MARQ is a superb example of how to bring ancient history alive. Its main galleries are filled with artefacts and treasures focusing respectively on prehistory, the Iberian civilization, the Romans and the Middle Ages. But the exhibits are only one part of the whole experience; most visitors will be fascinated by the state-of-the-art visual, light and sound effects. Videos show the crafts of tool-making and throwing pots, computer graphics bring the Roman past to life, Arab and medieval music echo through the galleries, and the lighting adds drama. **www.**marqalicante.com

➕ *Alicante 7e* ✉ Plaza Dr Gómez Ulla s/n ☎ 965 14 90 00 🕒 Jul–Aug Tue–Sat 11–2, 6–midnight, Sun 11–2; Jun–Sep Tue–Sat 10–7; Sun 10–2 🚌 2, 6, 9, 20, 23 🚉 Albufereta and San Juan served by Alicante–Dénia line ✋ Moderate

Parks

Alicante has two major parks, the Parque Monte Tossal, near the city's other castle, San Fernando, and El Palmeral, on the southern outskirts. Both are laid out with palms, trees and exotic plants and have good facilities for children.

➕ *Alicante 4e* (Parque Monte Tossal); *Alicante 3a, off map* (El Palmeral) ✋ All free 🍴 Bars at all locations (€) 🚌 All served by city buses

a walk around Alicante

Start at the east end of the tree-lined, tessellated Paseo Explanada de España (▶ 86) and cut north up Calle Cervantes into Plaza del Ayuntamiento, to emerge opposite the Town Hall (▶ 84) with its splendid façade and twin towers. Turn right along Calle de Jorge Juan then left up the steps to Plaza de Santa Maria.

The lovely Gothic church (▶ 86–87) is finely balanced by the Museo de la Asegurada.

Now take the Calle Villavieja left, downhill and turn right along Carrer de Maldonado and continue to Plaza del Carmen (currently undergoing restoration).

Plaza del Carmen is considered to be the heart of the Barrio Santa Cruz, the oldest part of Alicante.

Turn right, immediately left and look for Carrer San Rafael (signposted). A flight of steps takes you up through an area, adorned with flowers and lined with old houses. Near the top turn left into Carrer de Sant Antoni, then right up Calle Diputado Auset and follow the steps up to the Ermita de Santa Cruz.

The 19th-century Ermita lies just below the Torreón de la Ampollo, one of the old wall's surviving towers and offers fine panoramic views.

Retrace your steps, turn down Calle Marti, left down Carrer de Sant Lluis, Calle San Isidro and rejoin Carrer San Rafael to return to Plaza del Carmen. Follow the

road round to the right, then turn left down Calle Argensola into Plaza San Cristóbal. Another left turn along Carrer Llauradors, lined with 18th-century houses, leads to San Nicolás de Bari cathedral (➤ 86). Head west along Calle de Miguel Soler to Rambla de Méndez Núñez, then down to Paseo Explanada de España.

Distance 2km (1.2 miles)
Time 2–3 hours, depending on visits
Start/end point Paseo Explanada de España ✚ *Alicante 6b*
🚌 S, G, M
Lunch Darsena (€€) ✉ Muelle de Levante 6, Marina Deportiva
☎ 965 20 75 89

ORIHUELA

The ancient town of Orihuela makes a good target if you are aiming for a genuine historic inland town, unswamped by tourists, with a mix of impressive monuments, crumbling palaces and a gentle pace of life. Orihuela is easily reached from the coast so a visit here could be combined with a trip to Elche (Elx, ► 95–97) for a taste of untouched provincial Spain.

Called Aurariola by the Romans, the town stands in the lower reaches of the wonderfully fertile Segura valley, approached through a stately palm forest, Spain's second largest. From here, in the 15th century, Ferdinand and Isabella embarked on the final push for Granada to reclaim the city from the Moors. Later, the town became a wealthy Renaissance cathedral and university city, the commercial focus for the surrounding area.

In the 19th century, a combination of Alicante's (Alacant's) new role as regional capital and the devastation caused by a destructive earthquake diminished Orihuela's importance. Today the old churches, theatre, palaces and restored historic centre provide a backdrop to the everyday life of this prosperous inland town.

www.aytoorihuela.com

✚ 9E ✉ 60km (37 miles) southwest of Alicante

🍴 Choice of restaurants and bars 🚌 From Alicante

🚆 From Alicante ❓ Semana Santa (Mar/Apr); Moros y Cristianos (17 Jul); Virgen de Monserrat (8 Sep)

ℹ Palacio Rubalcava, Francisco Díez 25 ☎ 965 30 27 47

Catedral de San Salvador

This cathedral, with its nearby 18th-century bishop's palace, started life as a simple church, built between 1305 and 1355. Over the centuries alterations and additions have produced a wonderful mixture of styles, ranging from Romanesque through Catalan Gothic to baroque. The vaulted transept, built in 1500, is a high point, its bizarre, spirally twisted ribs rising to the shadows of the roof. More embellishments followed after the church became a cathedral in 1564; these include a richly carved choir, an ornate baroque organ and a couple of ambulatory chapels. The serene two-storey cloister, its honey-coloured arches enclosing a trim garden, was moved here after the Civil War. It contains the **Museo Diocesano del Arte Sacro,** a surprisingly rich collection which includes a Velázquez masterpiece, *The Temptation of St Thomas.*

✉ Calle Horno s/n ☎ 965 30 01 42
🕐 Mon–Fri 10–1:30, 5–7:30, Sat 10–1:30
✋ Free

Museo Diocesano del Arte Sacro
🕐 Mon–Fri 10:30–1:30, 4–6:30, Sat 10–1:30 ✋ Inexpensive

Colegio de Santo Domingo

Founded as a Dominican monastery and now a private school, Santo Domingo's architectural heyday coincided with its later role, from 1569 to 1824, as a university. During this time the three superb doorways were added to the main façade, and the elegant cloistered patios and sweeping panelled main staircase were built. Don't miss the refectory – its stunning *azulejo* frieze is one of the finest examples of this beautiful tile-work to be seen in this part of Spain.

✉ Calle Teruel 15 🕐 Mon–Fri 10–2, 4–7, Sat 10:30–1:30 🖐 Free

Iglesia de Santiago

This lovely Catalan Gothic church has a fine Isabelline-style front, the Puerto de Santiago, and a severe 16th-century nave and transept, dramatically punctuated by the opulence of the baroque Capilla Mayor and Salzillo's lyrical altarpieces.

✉ Plaza de la Merced 1 🕐 Mon–Fri 10:30–1:30, 5:30–7:30, Sat 10:30–1:30 🖐 Inexpensive

Santas Justa y Rufina

Near the splendid Renaissance town hall stands the austere and serene 14th-century church of Saints Justa and Rufina. Its gargoyled clock tower, the most southerly example of Catalan Gothic architecture, is one of the oldest buildings in Orihuela.

✉ Clavarana 🕐 Mon–Fri 10:30–1:30, 4–7 🖐 Inexpensive

Seminario de San Miguel

The old Seminario de San Miguel stands on the slopes of a hill above the town. It's worth the climb for the tranquillity and good views of the town and fertile plain, and a glimpse of the ruined castle above.

✉ Uphill from Plaza Caturia 🕐 Not open to the public

More to see around Alicante

BIAR

Steeped in history and dominated by its Moorish castle,
Biar is one of the most attractive of the ancient valley
towns that once guarded the Castilian border. The town,
a Moorish stronghold, was taken by Castile but fell to
Aragon in 1245 and became an important frontier post.
Today Biar is a charming town, and it is worth spending
time wandering about and soaking up the atmosphere.
Steep and narrow streets and peaceful plazas lead up to
the fortress, with its solid walls and magnificent free-
standing Moorish tower. There are fine valley views from
the **Castillo de Biar** and an interesting Gothic church
with later additions and a superb plateresque doorway.

➕ 18L ✉ 55km (34 miles) west of Alicante 🍴 Restaurants/
bars (€–€€) 🚌 From Alicante ❓ Moros y Cristianos (10–13 May)
ℹ️ Avenida de Villena 2 ☎ 965 81 11 77

Castillo de Biar

☎ 965 81 03 74 🕐 Tue–Fri 11–1, Sat 10–2, 4–6, Sun 10–2

CUEVAS DE CANALOBRE (COVES DE CANALOBRE)

The hills of Cabeçó d'Or, north of Alicante, are riddled
with caves and grottoes. This impressive limestone cavern, with
one of the highest vaults in Spain, has been skilfully illuminated to
show off the stalactites, stalagmites and strange limestone
formations. Among the many odd shapes is one known as the
canalobre, candelabra, from which the cave gets its name.

➕ 19H ✉ 24km (15 miles) north of Alicante and 40km (25 miles)
southwest of Benidorm ☎ 965 69 92 50 🕐 Jul–Sep daily 10:30–7:50;
Oct–Jun daily 11–5:50 🍴 Restaurant and bar (€–€€) ❓ Concerts are
sometimes held in the caves in summer; details from local tourist offices

ELCHE (ELX)

Surrounded and infiltrated by Europe's largest palm forest, the ancient city of Elche stands on the Vinalopó river. Spain's shoe-manufacturing capital, Elche is a stronghold of the Valencian language and one of the most historic towns in the region. It was founded as an Iberian settlement named Illici, and the Romans called it Iulia Illice Augusta. It became an important Visigothic episcopal centre, served as a major Moorish power base, was retaken by Jaime I in 1265 and has since quietly prospered. The old town, on the east bank of the river, contains almost everything worth seeing, so visitors can ignore the modern town, though some of the shoe factory outlets are worth visiting.

More than 300,000 palms grow in Elche, in verdant parks and shady squares and lining streets and gardens (➤ 44–45). The groves probably originated in Phoenician times and are protected by law. Many trees bear dates, and these are often for sale from street vendors. A miniature train tours the larger groves several times a day, or you can hire a bicycle and follow a mapped route through some of the plantations around the city's edge.

Elche's main sights are clustered around the vast baroque basilica of Santa María, whose blue-tiled dome dominates the ancient town centre. Built in the 16th and 17th centuries, the basilica, dark and cavernous inside and a mass of exuberant carving outside, is the scene in August of Elche's fiesta, the Misteri d'Elx. This medieval mystery play, celebrating in words and haunting music the death and assumption of the Virgin, has probably been performed by the townspeople since the 1260s, soon after the Reconquest. You can learn more about this at the **Museo Municipal de la Festa,** where the excellent audiovisual show gives some idea of the drama and beauty of the festival for which Elche is renowned.

Near the cathedral, Elche's **Museo Arqueológico** is housed in the Palacio Altamira. The collection includes some wonderful

Iberian pottery and stone pieces from the more important Museo Monográfico de Alcudia. This stands on the site of Illici, considered to be one of Spain's most important Iberian centres, a short distance outside Elche. The town centre has some fine Moorish remains. The Calaforra, or watchtower, is a remarkably complete building that has an extraordinary *mudéjar* hallway, while nearby, the 15th-century Renaissance façade of the **Convento de la Mercé** fronts a cloister and renovated 12th-century Arab baths.

From the centre of the city a pleasant stroll leads through the old Moorish quarter of Raval to the Franciscan monastery church of San José, where you can see *azejulos*, frescoes and carvings.

Elche is particularly noted for its festivals. Besides La Festa in August, Palm Sunday is a major celebration, with thousands of people, all dressed in new clothes, processing with palm branches through the palm trees themselves. Late December sees the Vinguda de la Mare de Déu, a procession from the sea to Elche, commemorating the legendary arrival of the text of the mystery play.

✚ 16H ✉ 23km (14 miles) southwest of Alicante 🍴 Choice of restaurants and bars (€–€€€) 🚌 From Alicante 🚆 From Alicante ❓ Semana Santa (Mar/Apr), Moros y Cristianos (1–8 Aug), Misteri d'Elx, La Festa (11–15 Aug), Vinguda de la Mare de Déu (28–29 Dec)

ℹ Parque Municipal ☎ 965 45 27 47

Museo Municipal de la Festa
✉ Carrer Major de la Vila 25 ☎ 965 45 34 64
🕐 Tue–Sat 10:30–1:30, 4:30–8 (Jul–Aug 5–9), Sun 10–1; audiovisual shows at 10:30, 11:30, 12:15, 5, 6, 7 (and 8 in summer) 💷 Moderate

Museo Arqueológico y de Historia de Elche
✉ Diagonal del Palau s/n ☎ 965 45 36 03
🕐 Tue–Sat 10–1:30, 4:30–8, Sun 10:30–1:30
💷 Inexpensive

Convento de la Mercé
🕐 Tue–Sat 10–1, 4:30–8:30, Sun 10–1 💷 Free

GUARDAMAR DEL SEGURA

Surrounded by citrus fruit orchards and fertile vegetable gardens, the ancient settlement of Guardamar, at the mouth of the Segura river, is a thriving small town and summer resort. Inhabited first by the Iberians as Cabero Lucero, the area was occupied by the Romans before becoming a major Moorish religious centre, known as Rábita Califal. The Christians ousted the Moors in the 13th century and built a castle and a church, and the village developed into a fishing and agricultural centre, its peace only disturbed by an 1829 earthquake, when it was rebuilt further away from the river. Guardamar is surrounded by the *dunas* – rolling sand dunes where you can take a camel ride. The beaches here are some of the loveliest on the coast (▶ 72–73). The spring and summer see a string of festivals; you can learn more local history at the **Museo Arqueológico,** and there is a market on Wednesday.

🚩 15G ✉ 40km (25 miles) south of Alicante 🍴 Restaurants and bars (€–€€€) 🛳 To Isla de Tabarca, Cruceros Tabarda ☎ 966 70 21 22

🛈 Contact tourist office for festival information
🛈 Plaza de la Constitución 7 ☎ 965 72 44 88
Museo Arqueológico, Etnológico y Palentológico Municipal
✉ Calle Colón 60, Casa de Cultura ☎ 965 72 86 10 🕐 Mon–Sat 10–5
✋ Inexpensive

HUERTO DEL CURA, ELCHE (ELX)
Best places to see, ➤ 44–45.

JIJONA (XIXONA)
Jijona, in the sierras behind Alicante (Alacant), is a mecca for the sweet-toothed. This everyday little town, with its old castle and narrow streets, is the home of *turrón*, an almond and honey-based nougat traditionally eaten at Christmas.

Probably of Moorish origin, its manufacture has a long history in Jijona and it is still produced by more than 30 small-scale family businesses on an artisan basis, with many of the production processes done by hand. It comes in a bewildering variety, ranging from soft and gooey through slightly crisp to tooth-cracking caramel, studded with glistening almonds. You can visit one of the genuine family businesses and there is a small museum, **Turrones el Lobo,** devoted to ancient production methods.

➕ 19J ✉ 22km (13.5 miles) north of Alicante 🍴 Restaurants/bars (€–€€€)
🚌 Bus from Alicante
Turrones el Lobo
✉ Alcoy 62 ☎ 965 61 01 25 🕐 Mon–Sat 10–1:30, 4–6:30

MONÓVAR (MONÒVER)

A visit to this thriving little town, rising from a green sea of rolling vineyards nestling within prime grape growing country, is a must for wine-lovers. The 19th century saw the strong, slightly sweet Monóvar reds fetching astronomical prices after *phylloxera* destroyed the French vineyards. Monastrel grapes are used for the reds, whose depth and strength comes from the *doble pasta* production method, where a first batch of grapes and must is mixed with a

second one in the same vat before fermentation begins. The excellent and delicate rosés owe their bouquet to another local method, where the wine is fermented from must drawn off from a first light crushing of the grapes. Sample, too, the perfumed and aromatic sweet dessert wine Fondillón, which needs 20 years to mature. Wine-tasting is available at Bodega Salvador Poveda.

🚩 16K 🖂 40km (25 miles) west of Alicante 🍴 Choice of restaurants and bars (€–€€€) 🚌 Bus from Alicante

NOVELDA

The town of Novelda, approached through a valley planted with vines and almonds, was one of the string of important Moorish fortress towns lining the inland valleys. Outside the town rises the Castillo de la Mola, whose superb 14th-century triangular tower was designed by Ibrahim of Tunis; stretches of ancient walling

still stand. Just below is the sanctuary of Santa Magdalena, a
Gaudí-influenced church. Other interesting buildings in town
include some fine Modernist houses, one of which contains the
fascinating local museum **Casa-Museo Modernista,** with stained
glass, period furniture and a fabulous spiral stairway.

✚ 16K ✉ 30km (18 miles) west of Alicante 🍴 Choice of restaurants and
bars (€–€€€) 🚌 Bus from Alicante ❓ Moros y Cristianos (mid-Jul); Santa
Magdalena (20 Jul and 7 Aug)

ℹ Calle Mayor 6 ☎ 965 60 92 28

Casa-Museo Modernista

✉ Calle Mayor 24 ☎ 965 60 02 37 🕐 Mon–Thu 9–2, 4–7 (Fri till 6),
Sat 11–2

SANTA POLA

Santa Pola functions both as the home of a huge Mediterranean fishing fleet and as a lively resort, with good sporting facilities, attractive buildings and a vibrant street market. South of the town stretch miles of clean sandy beaches backed by pines and eucalyptus. Behind the beaches the salt flats are a designated natural park, where you can spot flamingoes and a variety of birds of passage, as well as coastal flora. The town's fortress and two dilapidated watchtowers date from the mid-16th century, when fear of Berber pirate raids was high; the fortress now houses the town's cultural centre and the **Museo del Mar** (aquarium), its tanks holding a variety of fish and sea creatures. An audiovisual theatre features presentations on conservation which is fast becoming a priority along the coast. Well worth a visit for the daily afternoon fish market and for its agreeable summer street life, Santa Pola offers pavement cafés and a good range of excellent fish restaurants.

www.santapola.com

🚩 16G ✉ 18km (11 miles) south of Alicante 🍴 Restaurants/bars (€–€€€)
🚌 From Alicante ⛴ To Isla de Tabarca; daily in summer, Cruceros Tabardo
☎ 966 70 21 22 or Barco Santa Pola ☎ 965 41 11 13 ❓ Moros y Cristianos
(1–8 Sep)
ℹ Plaza Diputación 6 ☎ 966 69 22 76

Museo del Mar

✉ Plaza de Armas del Castillo ☎ 966 69 15 32 🕐 Apr–Sep Tue–Sat 11–1,
6:30–9:30, Sun 11–1, 4–7; Oct–Mar Tue–Sat 11–1, 4–7, Sun 11–1:30
👜 Moderate

SAX

The town of Sax, spreading down the hillside of the Vinalopó valley (► 106), is one of a picturesque chain of settlements dominated by castles, and is a good stopping point. The **Castillo de Sax** takes full advantage of its natural surroundings, the line of its walls following the contours of the limestone ridge on which it is built. The Moors first built a fortress here in the 10th century. The 12th-century Levante tower survives from this era but the two courtyards and fine three-storey keep are later. Sax, despite its superb defensive position, was finally taken by the Christians in the late 13th century. It then became part of the Marquisate of Villena until absorbed into the kingdom of Ferdinand and Isabella. The town's small Museo Arqueológico (archaeological museum) helps put this fascinating area into perspective.

✚ 17L 🖂 45km (28 miles) west of Alicante 🍴 Restaurant/bars (€–€€)
🚌 From Alicante 🚊 From Alicante ❓ Moros y Cristianos (1–5 Feb);
San Pancracio (1 May)

Castillo de Sax
☎ 965 47 40 06 for opening times and key; don't forget some form of ID

TABARCA

Boats run from several coastal towns to the Islote de la Cantera, a small group of islands where breezes blow even on the hottest days and the crystal-clear waters tempt snorkellers and divers. The main island is Tabarca, fortified and settled by Carlos III in the 18th century as a prison island for Genoese captives. The original walled town survives, with its stately entrance gate and church, but most summer visitors come here for the beaches, swimming and wonderful fish restaurants. The waters round the archipelago are a designated marine reserve, with some of the most interesting underwater life along the whole of the Costa Blanca. The shore base is in the old lighthouse, which you can visit on an island walk. It's best in the late afternoon when most visitors have gone.

🚩 16G 🖂 15km (9 miles) south of Alicante 🍴 Restaurants (€€–€€€)
🛥 From Alicante, Cruceros Kon Tiki (☎ 965 21 63 96); from Benidorm (also picks up from Calpe), Excursiones Marítima Benidorm (☎ 965 85 00 52); from Santa Pola, Cruceros Baeza-Paradi (☎ 608 33 04 22); from Guardamar, Cruceros Tabarca (☎ 966 70 21 22); from Torrevieja, Cruceros Tabarca (☎ 966 70 21 22)

TORREVIEJA

Torrevieja's distinctive low-level houses and wide streets date from its rebuilding after a catastrophic earthquake, though older buildings survive, including the remains of the Roman port. With its beaches, sports facilities, Museo de la Semana Santa, restaurants and summer nightlife, the town is a popular holiday centre. Spanish music fans flock here in August for the Habanera Festival, a celebration of the lilting songs brought back to the town from Cuba by the 19th-century salt exporters.

Torrevieja's salt flats are Europe's oldest and largest, sparkling flat expanses where salt water evaporates to produce pure sea salt, still widely exported. The salt flats at Torrevieja and La Mata are now also designated natural parks and have more than

250 recorded species of birds feeding on them. Find out more at the Museo del Mar y Sal.

✚ 9C ✉ 48km (30 miles) south of Alicante 🍴 Restaurants/bars (€–€€€)
🚌 From Alicante 🚆 From Alicante via Elche ⛴ To Isla de Tabarca, Cruceros Tabarca ☎ 966 70 21 22 ℹ Plaza Ruiz Capdepont s/n ☎ 965 70 34 33
❓ Real de la Feria (May), Virgen del Carmen (16 Jul)

VILLENA

This lively little town in the Vinalopó valley is dominated by La Atalaya, the water tower, a square-towered 15th-century castle. The original fortress was built by the Moors as one of a chain running up the valley, but Villena's history predates the Arabs by thousands of years. The **Museo Arqueológico** has collections spanning 8,000 years of early local history. Star attraction is the extraordinary gold hoard discovered nearby in the 1960s, whose solid gold pots, bowls, necklaces and bracelets date from around 3000BC. Other treasures come from nearby sites including the Bronze Age capital of the area, Cabeza Redonda. Villena's 16th-century church of Santiago is a must for Levantine Gothic enthusiasts. The font was carved by Jacopo Fiorentino, an assistant of Michelangelo, who settled here.

🟦 18L ✉ 60km (37 miles) west of Alicante 🍴 Restaurants and bars (€–€€€) 🚌 From Alicante 🚆 From Alicante ❓ Moros y Cristianos (4–9 Sep)

Museo Arqueológico

✉ Plaza de Santiago 1 ☎ 965 80 11 50, Ext 69 🕐 Tue–Fri 10–2, Sat–Sun 11–2 🖐 Inexpensive

VINALOPÓ VALLEY

The Vinalopó river gives its name to the valley running southwest from the hill country behind Alicante's coastline to the plains. The valley was frontier territory for Carthaginians and Romans, Moors and Christians, and the rising new powers of Castile and Aragon in the years following the Reconquest. A chain of defensive castles testifies to these times and a drive up the valley gives you a chance to explore them. There are castles at Aspe, Novelda (► 100–101), Monforte del Cid (Monforte del Sit), Elda, Petrel (Petrer) and Sax (► 103), with Biar (► 94) a little to the north.

🟦 16J ✉ Starts 30km (18.5 miles) west of Alicante 🍴 Restaurants everywhere (€–€€) 🚌 From Alicante

HOTELS

ALICANTE (ALACANT)
Almirante (€€)
On the seafront at San Juan, this is an ideal choice for watersports enthusiasts. Good restaurant, friendly staff and tranquillity.

✉ Avenida Niza 38 ☎ 965 65 01 12; www.hotelalmirante.com

Eurostars Mediterránea Plaza (€€€)
Stylish, comfortable hotel in the centre of the old town, facing the Ayuntamiento and a stone's throw from the sea – there are lovely views of the old quarter and the castle from virtually every room.

✉ Pl de Ayuntamiento 6 ☎ 965 21 01 88: www.hotelmediterraneaplaza.com

Hostal Les Monges Palace (€€)
Situated in the old part of town, this hotel is a real gem. Tastefully decorated with antiques, paintings and tiles, each room has an individual style. The suite has a jacuzzi and sauna.

✉ San Agustin 4 ☎ 965 21 50 46; www.lesmonges.es

Rambla (€€)
Convenient, centrally situated budget hotel with pleasant rooms, some with a balcony overlooking a wide avenue leading to the sea. Excellent value.

✉ Rambla Méndez Núñez 9 ☎ 965 14 45 80; www.hotelrambla.com

Sidi San Juan (€€€)
The ultimate in resort hotels just north of the city centre. Views, three pools and access to the beach through manicured grounds.

✉ Pda Cabo La Huerta, Playa de San Juan ☎ 965 16 13 00; www.hotelessidi.es

ALCOY (ALCOI)
Mas de Pau (€€)
This beautifully restored 18th-century granary stands in lovely country 9km (5.5 miles) east of Alcoy. Rather small rooms, but worth it for the pool, restaurant and ambience.

✉ Carretera Alcoy-Penáguila, Km 9 ☎ 965 51 31 11

BIAR
Vilá de Biar (€€)
Delightful hotel with elegant public rooms and lovely views. It incorporates the palace of the viscounts of Valdesoto.
✉ San José 2 ☎ 902 22 00 52; www.fanecaes-alicante.com

ELCHE (ELX)
Candelijas (€€)
A good, central, family-run budget choice, with clean, well-equipped rooms, all with bathrooms and air-conditioning, and a lift.
✉ Doctor Ferrán 19 ☎ 965 46 65 12

Huerto del Cura (€€€)
A luxurious and traditional hotel, affiliated to the state *paradors*, set in the middle of Elche's palm groves and opposite the famous garden. Lovely grounds, every facility and an excellent restaurant.
✉ Porta de la Morera 14 ☎ 966 61 00 11; www.huertodelcura.com

GUARDAMAR
Edén Mar (€€)
Summer season, excellent budget hotel. Near the beach, within easy walk of bars and restaurants, and all rooms have bathrooms.
✉ Avenida Mediterráneo 19 ☎ 965 72 92 13

Meridional (€€€)
Holiday hotel, right on the beach. No pool, but tennis, satellite TV and friendly staff. Rooms have balconies with sea views.
✉ Urbanización Dunas de Guardamar ☎ 965 72 83 40; www.hotelmeridional.es

ORIHUELA
Melia Boutique Palacio de Tudemir (€€€)
Lovely hotel housed in a beautifully restored 18th-century palace in the historic heart of Orihuela. A grand staircase topped by a brilliant dome is a feature. Facilities and service in keeping with a hotel of this calibre.
✉ Alfonso XIII 1 ☎ 965 73 80 10; www.solmelia.com

SANTA POLA
Pola-Mar (€€€)
Large hotel, right on the seafront next to the port and sailing club. Popular with Spanish families; good restaurant and lovely views.
✉ Playa de Levante 6 ☎ 965 41 30 20

TABARCA
Casa del Gobernador (€€)
A wonderful hotel in the restored 18th-century governor's house.
✉ Calle Arzola 2, Isla de Tabarca ☎ 965 96 08 86;
www.casadelgobernador.com

TORREVIEJA
Lloyds Club (€€€)
An apartment hotel with a restaurant and pool in a superb beach-side position. Tastefully furnished and well-equipped apartments.
✉ Avenida de los Holandeses 2 ☎ 966 92 00 00

Masa Internacional (€€€)
This pretty and comfortable hotel, a little outside town, would suit people wanting to escape Torrevieja's frenetic summer evenings.
✉ Avenida Alfredo Nobel 150 ☎ 966 92 15 37

VILLENA
Salvadora (€€)
An old-fashioned hotel, with better facilities than its one-star rating would imply. Excellent restaurant specializing in local dishes.
✉ Avenida de la Constitución 102 ☎ 965 80 09 50;
www.hotelsalvadora.com

RESTAURANTS

ALICANTE (ALACANT)
Azahar (€€€)
The chef and maître d' from one of Alicante's oldest restaurants branched out here on their own, and the years of experience certainly show in the excellent cooking and attention to detail.
✉ C/ Alberola 57 ☎ 965 12 13 48 ⏰ Lunch daily, dinner Fri–Sat

El Bocaito (€€)
See page 76.

Botanero (€€)
Mexican restaurant with a long bar and a new, modern concept, serving Mexican-style dishes with Spanish influences. Later in the evening the place virtually reverts to a cocktail bar. Fridays and Saturdays can be particularly lively after midnight when there is music and dancing.

✉ Bailén 3 ☎ 965 20 38 56 🕐 Lunch and dinner

El Buen Comer (€€)
Fancy restaurant upstairs with excellent fish and grilled meat options. The downstairs bar and *terraza* is more economical and also reliably good. Try the sea bass baked in salt.

✉ Calle Mayor 8 ☎ 965 21 35 41 🕐 Lunch and dinner

El Cantó (€)
See page 58.

César Anca (€€)
A friendly pub-style restaurant, where the simple and appetizing food is prepared with an up-to-date twist. Excellent service.

✉ General Lacy 12 ☎ 965 12 43 62 🕐 Closed Mon pm, Sun and all Jul

Ibéricos (€€)
Quality restaurant featuring dishes based on pork. There's a long bar festooned with hanging hams and stocked with an interesting array of *tapas*, which could include a pigs tail, ear or various other parts of the animal.

✉ Calle Gerona 5 ☎ 965 21 30 08 🕐 Lunch and dinner. Closed Sun

El Jardín de Galicia (€€€)
In the heart of town, specializing in traditional cooking from the region of Galicia, from where much of the excellent meat and shellfish comes.

✉ Maisonnave 33 ☎ 965 12 01 61 🕐 Lunch and dinner. Closed Sun

Jumillano (€€€)

Long-established *méson*-style restaurant and one of Alicante's finest, serving impeccably cooked and presented local dishes.
✉ César Elguezábal 64 ☎ 965 21 29 64 🕙 Closed Sun pm

El Lugar (€)

Local cooking using the freshest ingredients. Popular with locals.
✉ García Morato 4 ☎ 965 14 11 31 🕙 Lunch and dinner. Closed Sun and public hols

Maestral (€€)

An old-established upmarket restaurant, specializing in rice dishes and shellfish, as well as some international specialities.
✉ Andalucía 18 ☎ 965 26 25 85 🕙 Lunch and dinner. Closed Sun pm

Nou Manolin (€€)

Very popular bar and restaurant serving the best of Alicante and Spanish cooking. Rice and shellfish, with good wine list.
✉ Villegas 3 ☎ 965 20 03 68 🕙 Lunch and dinner

Piripi (€€)

See page 77.

Rosa (€)

See page 59.

Tragallum (€€)

The chef uses local ingredients and traditions; dishes include rabbit with pine-nuts and parsley, and fine terrines spiked with rosemary.
✉ Poeta Campos Vasallo 33 ☎ 965 21 38 69 🕙 Lunch and dinner. Closed Sun pm and Mon

Valencia Once (€)

Bar-restaurant with a menu packed with Alicante dishes and some of the best puddings in town. Very popular, so it's best to book.
✉ Valencia 11 ☎ 965 21 13 09 🕙 Lunch and dinner. Closed Sun and Mon pm, Easter week and mid-Aug to mid-Sep

ELCHE (ELX)
Asador Ilicitano (€€)

A rustic restaurant offering a taste of Castile – huge roasts, suckling pig, hearty bean dishes and fine hams, as well as fish.
✉ Maestro Giner 9 ☎ 965 43 58 64 ⏱ Lunch and dinner. Closed Sun and 15–30 Aug

Casa Enrique (€)

See page 58.

Doña Ana (€)

Succulent grilled meats, fish and shellfish. On weekdays they also offer a good-value *menú del dia*.
✉ Dr Caro 17 ☎ 965 44 44 94 ⏱ Lunch and dinner. Closed Sun

El Parque (€)

Big and busy restaurant in the centre of Elche's magnificent palm forest. The décor is functional but the food spot-on.
✉ Parque Municipal ☎ 965 45 34 15 ⏱ Lunch and dinner

GUARDAMAR DEL SEGURA
Rincón de Pedro (€)

A cheerful, lively atmosphere, big terrace and good range of traditional rice and fish dishes.
✉ Cibeles 2, Urbanización las Dunas ☎ 965 72 80 95 ⏱ Lunch and dinner. Closed Wed

MONÓVAR (MONÒVER)
Casa Elias (€€)

Inland rice dishes and traditional, country-style home cooking.
✉ Rosales 7, Cinorlet ☎ 966 97 95 17 ⏱ Lunch only. Closed Wed

Xiri (€€)

The food has character and uses fresh local ingredients in its rice and pasta dishes. Excellent selection of the best local wines.
✉ Parque Alameda s/n ☎ 965 47 29 10 ⏱ Lunch and dinner. Closed Sun pm, Mon and 20 Feb–15 Mar

ORIHUELA

Ateneo (€€)

Elegant establishment, tiled with a predominance of blue tones. The cafetería/restaurant is basic, popular with locals, and offers a good selection of *tapas* and a reasonably priced menu of the day.

✉ Arzobispo Loaces ☎ 965 30 40 18 🕙 Lunch and dinner. Closed Sun pm and Mon

Casa Corro (€)

Functional, but excellent restaurant near Orihuela's palm forest, with the accent on regional cooking.

✉ Avenida Doctor García Rogel s/n, Palmeral de San Antón ☎ 965 30 29 63 🕙 Lunch and dinner. Closed Mon pm and second two weeks of Aug

SANTA POLA

Batiste (€€)

A pretty restaurant, situated in a flower-filled garden right beside the sea, offering shellfish, rice and fish, and an excellent wine list.

✉ Pérez Ojeda 6 ☎ 965 41 14 85 🕙 Lunch and dinner

Casa Joaquín (€)

Located near the port, this popular little restaurant is known for its fresh seafood and tasty rice dishes.

✉ Félix de Rodríguez de la Fuente ☎ 965 41 12 82 🕙 Lunch and dinner

La Goleta (€€)

A nautically themed tavern offering great rice recipes from the island of Tabarca. The fish and shellfish are wonderfully fresh and there is a lively atmosphere.

✉ Hernán Cortés 6 ☎ 966 69 30 63 🕙 Lunch and dinner. Closed Mon (except Jul and Aug), and two weeks in Oct/Nov

Miramar (€€)

An elegant summer restaurant with a big terrace and friendly service. Local rice and fish, with lots of vegetables and the freshest of salads.

✉ Pérez Ojeda s/n ☎ 965 41 38 96 🕙 Lunch and dinner

Palomar (€€)

The Palomar produces the best of local rice and seafood dishes. Enjoy them right beside the beach on the terrace of this bustling restaurant.

✉ Playa de Levante s/n ☎ 965 41 32 00 🕐 Lunch and dinner

TORREVIEJA

Bahía (€)

Good range of seafood and international dishes.

✉ Avenida Libertad 3 ☎ 965 71 39 94 🕐 Lunch and dinner. Closed Mon

Brisas del Mar (€)

Popular restaurant with terrace; some unusual local dishes such as *caldero* (rice cooked in a well-flavoured stock made from shellfish and seafood).

✉ Paseo Vista Alegre 10 ☎ 965 70 52 01 🕐 Lunch and dinner. Closed Mon pm

Cabo Roig (€€)

Pleasantly situated restaurant on Cabo Roig, with the benefit of a large summer terrace.

✉ Urbanización Cabo Roig s/n, Carretera Torrevieja–Cartagena Km 8 ☎ 966 76 02 90 🕐 Lunch and dinner

Miramar (€€)

Specializes in inventive seafood and rice dishes.

✉ Paseo Vista Alegre ☎ 965 71 34 15 🕐 Lunch and dinner. Closed Tue and Dec–Jun

Restaurante Vegetariano (€€)

Imaginative (and rare for Spain) vegetarian restaurant run by a Spanish-Australian couple.

✉ Calle Pedro Lorca 13 ☎ 966 70 66 83 🕐 Closed Mon

El Rincón de las Jarres (€€)

See page 59.

VILLENA
La Teja Azul (€€)
Cosy rustic atmosphere with brick and beam interior. Try the house speciality *arroz a banda*, a filling rice dish.

✉ Calle Sancho Medina 34 ☎ 965 34 82 34 ⏱ Lunch and dinner. Closed Tue

Wary Nessy (€)
Excellent family-run restaurant specializing in dishes peculiar to Villena; bar food and good local wines.

✉ Isabel la Católica 13A ☎ 965 80 10 47 ⏱ Lunch and dinner. Closed Mon and second two weeks in Jul

SHOPPING

ARTS AND CRAFTS
Artesania
An interesting shop carrying a large, attractive range of ceramics, pottery and other crafts from the Alicante region.

✉ V Pascual Alfonso X el Sabio 15, Alicante (Alacant) ☎ 965 14 01 39

MB Cerámica Artística
Tiny shop in the town centre with a delightful display of ceramics. Unusual designs, tastefully blending modern and traditional.

✉ Calle Mayor 31, Alicante ☎ 965 21 99 38

BOOKS
Librería Europa
Extensive bookshop with a large variety of topics, maps, travel guides and a wide-ranging selection of titles in English and other European languages.

✉ Calle Oscar Espla 2, Calpe ☎ 965 83 58 24

DEPARTMENT STORES
El Corte Inglés
Spain's most famous department store with an enormous selection of goods, ranging from quality fashionwear in leather and suede to ceramics, Toledo work and a range of gifts.

✉ Avenida Maissonnaves 53 and Federico Soto 1–3 ☎ 965 92 50 01

FASHION AND JEWELLERY

Bernardino
Wide selection of men's and women's shoes from this Elche-based manufacturer.

✉ San Miguel 16 ☎ 965 45 21 93; Diagonal 5, Elche (Elx) ☎ 965 43 63 89

Botticelli
Exquisite leather handbags and shoes; one of a chain of three in town.

✉ Gran Via s/n, Alicante ☎ 965 24 01 65

Boutique Bolé Bolé
A ladies' clothes shop with a good range of classic and not-so-classic designs.

✉ Plaza Ruperto Chapí 6, Alicante ☎ 965 14 30 33

Joyería Gómez
A chic jeweller with some attractive and typically Spanish designs. Good range of international watches.

✉ Corredora 6, Elche ☎ 965 45 28 50

Salvador Artesano
Out-of-town factory outlet for one of Elche's main shoe and leather manufacturers. Search through for some amazing bargains.

✉ Carretera Murcia–Alicante Km 53, Apto 504, Elche (Elx) ☎ 966 67 54 41

FOOD AND DRINK

Bodega Selección
An attractive wineshop that is well stocked with over 400 different Spanish wines, cavas and liqueurs. Also imported specialities.

✉ Avenida Constitución 22A, Orihuela ☎ 965 81 37 81

Convento de la Trinidad
Spanish nuns maintain the old tradition of cake, sweet and pastry making here, using local recipes and the finest ingredients. Sample traditional delicacies from Orihuela; just give your order and the goodies will appear on a turn-table.

✉ Convento de la Trinidad, Plaza de la Trinidad, Orihuela ☎ No phone (enclosed order)

Damas
A wonderful bar and *pastelería*, with an huge range of sweet and savoury creations.
✉ Pintor Lorenzo Casanova 5, Alicante ☎ 965 12 14 71

Enacoteca Bernadino
More than 2,500 Spanish vintages on offer, specializing in Rioja.
✉ Calle Alberola 38, Alicante ☎ 965 28 08 73

Espí
Stock up on *turrón* (almond confection) at this old-fashioned speciality shop in the centre.
✉ Lopéz Torregrosa 17, Alicante ☎ 965 21 44 41

ENTERTAINMENT

BARS AND NIGHTCLUBS

El Caribe
A hip-swinging Latino club with salsa and merengue.
✉ Calle General Primo de Riera 14, Alicante (Alacant) ☎ 965 20 77 85
🕐 Tue–Thu 8:30pm–3am, Fri–Sat 10:30pm–4:30am

Discoteca Camelot
Features all the latest music and dance crazes.
✉ Avenida de Elche 38, Santa Pola ☎ None 🕐 Daily 11pm–6am

Havana
Lively bar by day; even livelier dance space by night.
✉ Rambla Ménez Núñez 26, Alicante (Alacant) ☎ 965 21 69 26 🕐 Sun–Thu 8am–1am

Pachá
Lively disco on one of the town's main streets.
✉ Calle Haroldo Parres 6, Alicante (Alacant) ☎ 965 21 19 38 🕐 Daily 11pm–6am

THEATRE AND CONCERTS
Gran Teatro
Mixed programme of theatre, classical music and films in Spanish.
✉ Kurshal 2, Elche (Elx) ☎ 965 45 14 03

Teatro Circo
A wide range of concerts, theatre and shows for Spanish-speakers, housed in a beautifully restored turn-of-the-20th-century circular theatre.
✉ Plaza Poeta Sansano 1, Orihuela ☎ 966 74 01 04

Teatro Principal
✉ Plaza Ruperto Chapí s/n, Alicante (Alacant) ☎ 965 20 31 00; www.teatroprincipaldealicante.com

SPORT

GOLF
Club de Golf Alenda
✉ Autovía Alicante–Madrid Km 15, Alicante (Alacant) ☎ 965 62 05 21

Club de Golf Villa Martín
✉ Carretera Alicante–Cartagena Km 50, Orihuela ☎ 966 76 51 27

HORSE-RIDING
Club Hípico de Campoamor
✉ Carretera Cartagena–Alicante Km 48, Alicante (Alacant) ☎ 965 32 12 38

SAILING
Club Náutico Costa Blanca
✉ Avenida de la Condomina 20, Alicante (Alacant) ☎ 965 15 44 91

Club Náutico de Santa Pola
✉ Muella de Poniente s/n, Santa Pola ☎ 965 41 24 03

Benidorm and the North

The name Benidorm is familiar worldwide, synonymous with packed beaches, high-rise hotels, glitz and fun, a place where millions of visitors let their hair down and enjoy good-value sunshine holidays.

□ Benidorm

Most never stir from the town itself, but for those who do there are huge rewards. Other lively resorts lie on the coast to the north and south, easily reached by the little train which trundles up and down between Alicante (Alacant) and Dénia.

Altea, Calpe (Calp), Jávea (Xàbia) and Dénia are all worth visiting for a change of scene and pace, and a chance to discover the more traditional resorts.

Inland from Benidorm rise some of Spain's most steep and beautiful coastal mountains. This area, dotted with historic towns and villages, planted with almonds, oranges and olives, preserves a way of life untouched by the development of the last 40 years.

BENIDORM

Benidorm, the Mediterranean's largest tourist resort, is a shining example of a superbly organized popular destination, and no one should criticize the slickness and efficiency of the operation, which truly provides 'something for everyone'. Winter and summer alike, Benidorm has got the formula right for visitors of every age.

The earliest known settlement in Benidorm dates back to the second Iberian epoch, with Roman influences. As it developed, through fishing and agriculture, its castle was constantly attacked by pirates from North Africa and the Berber coast. By the 1600s this threat had diminished, the parish church was built, and the fishermen were acquiring an international reputation as tuna fishers. The town became one of many similar coastal settlements, and it was not until the late 19th century that the attractions of its micro-climate began to be known. The first tourists were Spanish, who came in increasing, but still minimal, numbers up to the 1950s. More leisure and higher incomes coincided with cheaper air travel, and throughout the 1960s Benidorm's growth was spectacular. Hotels, apartment buildings, shops, restaurants and recreational facilities proliferated, the Spanish learned what foreign holiday-makers expected, and Benidorm's economic future was assured.

Today, Benidorm can provide everything you need on holiday, or make a good base from which to explore inland. ⊞ 21G 🛈 Carnaval (Feb), Fallas de San José (16–19 Mar), Semana Santa (Mar/Apr), Festa de la Creu (1 May), Hogueras de San Juan (24 Jun), San Fermín (6–7 Jul), Virgen del Carmen (16 Jul), San Jaime (25 Jul), Moros y Cristianos (end Sep), Fiestas Patronales (mid Nov) 🛈 Avenida Martinez Alejos 6 ☎ 965 85 32 24

Castillo-Mirador

Nothing remains of Benidorm's castle, thought to have been built before the town's first charter was issued in 1325. It was strategically sited at the highest point of the original settlement on the promontory now occupied by the old village. It was repeatedly attacked by Algerian and Berber pirates. Plaintive documents exist imploring the king for money to repair it throughout the 16th century. It was blown up in 1812 and its ruins had disappeared by the beginning of the 20th century. Its old site, now a charming square by a church, is a favourite look-out point with sweeping views of Benidorm's superb beaches.
✉ Plaza de Castillo 🍴 Several bars on the square

Iglesia de San Jaime

St James is the parish church of Benidorm, beautifully sited on the old town's promontory overlooking the sea. Building started in 1740, the same year as the discovery of the statue of Our Lady of the Sorrows, the town's patron saint. At this date Benidorm was expanding considerably on tuna-fishing profits, which helped fund the church's construction. With its blue-tiled domes and white walls, it is typical of all traditional churches along the coast, and for local people is still very much the heart of the town.

✉ Plaza Castelar ⏰ Currently closed for restoration ✋ Free

La Isla de Benidorm

A mere 20-minute boat trip across the bay, Benidorm Island makes a good destination for a picnic and swim. Rising at one end to sheer cliffs, its clear deep waters are ideal for snorkelling and scuba diving. The island is uninhabited except for gulls and other seabirds, and is a designated sanctuary. You can get there in an 'aquascope' boat, whose transparent hull lets you see underwater.

🍴 Summer-only bar 🚢 Excursiones Marítimo Benidorm, Puerto de Benidorm ☎ 965 85 00 52 ⏰ Every 45 minutes 10–6

Parque de l'Aigüera

Benidorm is justly proud of Aigüera Park, a long sweep of promenades and greenery running seawards down a dried-up river valley. It was the first major piece of public architecture in Benidorm, designed to add some sophistication to a resort that was tired of being seen essentially as a sun-and-sand destination. It succeeded brilliantly: its elegant central avenue acts as a meeting place and its two fine amphitheatres, dramatically lit at night, are ideal for concerts and cultural events.

✉ Avenida de l'Aigüera 🖐 Free 🍴 Bars (€)

Playa de Levante

Backed by towering hotels, the curve of golden sand known as the Playa de Levante is full day and night. For most visitors the beach epitomizes Benidorm's attractions – hot sun, clear blue water, clean sand. It also offers wonderful chances to make friends from all over the world, to show off, and to indulge in some serious people-watching yourself. At night it's transformed into a brilliantly sparkling chain of lights, the perfect backdrop for the resort's vibrant night scene.

✉ Avenida d'Alcoi/Avenida de Madrid 🍴 Choice of restaurants and bars nearby

Playa de Poniente

Poniente is Benidorm's other beach, just as clean and beautiful as Levante and situated on the other side of the old town. Its promenade, currently being rebuilt and modernized to create a wider footpath with less traffic, is also thronged for the evening *paseo* and glitters with a myriad lights at night.

✉ Avenida de la Armada Española 🍴 Choice of restaurants and bars nearby

a walk around Benidorm

Start at the seafront at the corner of Avenida d'Alcoi, Playa de Levante, and walk up Avenida Martínez Alejos to Plaça de la Creu. A left turn brings you into the old town of Benidorm.

The small palm tree, la Palmera, on your right, is a popular meeting place for local inhabitants. Stroll along the pedestrianized avenue known as La Alameda, attractively tree-lined and crammed with shops.

Continue up Calle Mayor. Pass under the arch to the pretty clifftop square of Plaça del Castell, attractively decorated with tiles and dominated by the blue-domed church of San Jaime (▶ 122).

Stroll around to admire the stunning views over Benidorm, with Playa de Levante (▶ 123) backed by the dramatic promontory of the Sierra Helada to the left, and Playa de Poniente (▶ 123) to the right.

Turn south to Plaça de la Senyoria and take the flight of steps down to the harbour. Then take a right turn along along the Paseo de la Carretera.

This is another lively pedestrianized street, humming with activity, lined with shops and tiny side streets filled with tempting bars and cafés.

A left fork into Calle de las Herrerías will lead you to Benidorm's impressive new Ayuntamiento (City Hall) set in the Parque de l'Aigüera (➤ 123). Walk up through the park to take a look at the Plaza de Toros and retrace your steps down through the park, cross over into Calle Arco Iris and complete the walk in the Plaza de la Hispanidad (known as El Triangular).

Distance 2.5km (1.5 miles)

Time 1.5–2 hours

Start point Avenida d'Alcoi 🚌 3, 12

End point Plaza de la Hispanidad 🚌 3, 12

Lunch La Cuina de Ponent (€€) ✉ Calle Vicente Llorca Alos 13 ☎ 966 80 70 63

JÁTIVA (XÀTIVA)

The ancient settlement of Játiva lies less than an hour from the coast. Here the Iberians prospered and minted coinage, only to be ousted first by the Romans and then by Hannibal's Carthaginians on their way to Rome. A Visigothic episcopal seat, the town was conquered by the Moors in the 10th century, and it was from Játiva that they introduced paper manufacture to Europe. Jaime I took the town in 1244 and its fortunes waxed and waned over the following centuries. Burned in 1707, it was rebuilt but gradually lost its political importance. The birth-place of two Borgia popes (born 'Borja' in Spain) and the painter El Españoleto, Játiva today offers a perfect contrast to the modern coastal resorts.

The best way to get a feel of the town is to walk, following the

route marked on the useful leaflet you can pick up at the tourist office. The old quarter, its streets lined with stately mansions, runs along the side of the hill that overlooks the whole town. A road runs up this hill to the magnificent castle (➤ opposite), occupying virtually the entire ridge, and goes past the lovely early church of San Feliu (Sant Feliu, ➤ 50–51). It's a tough walk, so the twice-daily tourist train might prove useful. The wonderful panoramic views from the top of the hill help to explain Játiva's historical and strategic importance through the centuries.

Back down the hill an attractive and broad avenue lined with plane trees divides the historic centre of Játiva from the modern town.

✚ 22M ✉ 110km (68 miles) nothwest of Benidorm 🍴 Choice of restaurants and bars (€–€€€) 🚍 From Alicante ℹ Alameda de Jaume I 50 ☎ 962 27 33 46; www.infoxativa.com

El Castell

This huge fortress, stretching along a ridge, dominates the town. Actually two castles, one pre-Roman and one later, its towered walls are still impressive and it's easy to see why it was considered one of the most secure in the region. The section known as the lower castle is the older, the majority of its surviving walls and towers built by the Moors. It occupies the site of the Iberian, Roman and Carthaginian fortress and some sections of the stonework date from Roman times. The Queen's Tower is said to be named after Hannibal's wife, who gave birth to a son here. The upper castle is much larger; a confusing succession of ancient gateways, crumbling courtyards, guardrooms and towers. Highlights are the tiny and beautiful Gothic chapel of Santa María, reconstructed in 1431 on an earlier site, and a series of Arabic cisterns and watchtowers. The view from the highest point is well worth the climb; the town lies directly below, with ranges of hills to the south and the ancient frontier with Castile to the east.

✉ Carretera Castillo ☎ 962 27 42 74 🕐 May–Sep Tue–Sun 10–7; Oct–Apr Tue–Sun 10–6 👋 Moderate 🍴 Bar within castle walls (€) 🚍 Tourist train from outside tourist office Mon–Sat 12:30, 4:30; Sun 12, 1, 4:30 ❓ Occasional summer concerts – ask at tourist office

Museo l'Almodi

Housed in the mid-16th-century municipal granary, Játiva's town museum is worth a visit for the building alone. The Gothic façade hides a spacious Renaissance interior built around a graceful columned courtyard, all imaginatively restored as a backdrop for the collections. The archaeological treasures include Iberian and Roman artefacts and some fine Moorish ceramics and fragments of buildings. The picture collection has paintings by José Ribera, later known as El Españoleto, born here in 1591, and a loan collection of mainly 17th-century works from the Prado in Madrid. Look for the Goya engravings and the portrait of Philip V, hung permanently upside down in retribution for his burning of Játiva during the War of the Spanish Succession.

✉ Corretgeria 46 ☎ 962 27 65 97 🕐 Mid-Jun to mid-Sep Tue–Fri 10–2:30, Sat–Sun 10–2; mid-Sep to mid-Jun Tue–Fri 10–2, 4–6, Sat–Sun 10–2 ✋ Moderate

The Old Town

As you wander the peaceful streets of the old town, there are some wonderful churches and buildings to admire, many dating from Játiva's rebuilding after Philip V burned the town in 1707. Among them is the collegiate church of La Seu, built with Borja money in 1596, a vast Renaissance structure with a

Gothic nave. Opposite stands the Hospital Real, dating from the 15th century, its lovely façade adorned with a ring of beautifully carved angels encircling the Madonna over the main door. Look out, too, for the Romanesque church of San Francisco, Sant Pere and the house where Borja Pope Alexander II was born. Other fine mansions include the Palacio del Marqués de Montortal, a lovely 15th-century building with later additions, and the 19th-century Casa de Diego. The old town's streets are punctuated with little plazas, many of them filled with the sound of splashing water from the numerous fountains. The simple one in the tiny plaza outside the Palace of Justice is Gothic in style and the town's only medieval fountain. On the edge of the old quarter you'll find the Font de las 25 Canelles, a fountain erected in 1794 with 25 spouts. Surprises are around every corner – peaceful squares and graceful mansions, with the added attraction that few tourists have yet discovered Játiva.

San Feliu (Sant Feliu)
Best places to see,
➤ 50–51.

More to see in the North

AGRES

Agres is a quiet upland agricultural village, set around an ancient convent and a castle. It makes a good jumping-off point for exploring the Sierra de Mariola, the Gallinera valley (➤ 40–41), and inland towns such as Alcoy (➤ below) and Biar (➤ 94). The surrounding hills are wonderful walking country, carpeted with wild herbs and dotted with *pozos de nieve*, medieval ice-houses.

➕ 20L 🖂 65km (40 miles) northwest of Alicante 🍴 Restaurants/bars (€–€€) 🚌 From Alicante and Alcoy ❓ Mare de Deu de Agres (1–9 Sep); San Miguel (29 Sep)

ℹ️ Ayuntamiento de Agres ☎ 965 51 00 01

ALCOY (ALCOI)

Modern Alcoy stands on a promontory, first settled by the Iberians, between the rivers Molonar and Barchell, its houses tumbling

down the sides of a gorge. It's the largest industrial centre in the area, a solid, prosperous and seemingly dour town, worth seeing for its position and fine 19th-century architecture. Centred around the grandiose Plaza de España (Plaça d'Espanya) and the arcaded Plaza de Dins (Plaça de Dins), Alcoy is scattered with baroque churches and civic buildings, dating mainly from the end of the 19th century. The money came from cotton, still processed here, and was spent on extending the 17th-century city, and building the five bridges across the gorge.

The town has the fascinating **Museo de Fiestas** where the costumes used in the Moros y Christianos festival are stored. This rumbustious event celebrates a Christian victory over the Moors in

1279, when Saint George came to the aid of the inhabitants, and is a source of huge local pride. The Museu Arqueológico Municipal has a good local collection, which includes some Iberian treasures.

✚ 20K ✉ 48km (30 miles) northwest of Alicante ⬛ Choice of restaurants and bars (€–€€€) 🚌 From Alicante 🚆 From Alicante ❓ Moros y Cristianos (22–24 Apr)

ℹ San Lorenzo 2 ☎ 965 53 71 55

Museo de Fiestas

✉ San Miguel 62 ☎ 965 54 05 80 🕐 Aug Mon–Fri 10:30–1:30; Jul Mon–Fri 11–1, 5:30–7:30; Sep–Jun Tue–Fri 11–1, 5:30–7:30, Sat, Sun 10:30–1:30 💷 Inexpensive

ALTEA

Sheltered and encircled by steep hills and cliffs, Altea tumbles
down the slopes below the blue-tiled domed church of La Virgen
de la Consuelo, sitting at the highest point of the picturesque old
village like a cherry on a cake. A Roman settlement, the original
fishing village was restored by a colony of artists in the 1950s and
a variety of painters, craftsmen and potters are still among its
inhabitants. Their sense of style spills over into the steep white
streets, shaded by orange trees, festooned with geraniums and

lined with tempting boutiques. Inevitably such charms, and Altea's proximity to Benidorm, attract huge numbers of visitors. The beach is backed by a pleasant palm-lined esplanade with a wide range of restaurants, and there are good watersports facilities.

➕ 21G ✉ 12km (7.5 miles) north of Benidorm 🍴 Restaurants/bars (€–€€€) 🚌 From Benidorm 🚆 From Benidorm ❓ Fogueres de Sant Joan (24 Jun), San Pedro (Jul/Aug), Moros y Cristianos (last week of Sep)

ℹ️ Calle San Pedro 9 ☎ 965 84 41 14

BENISSA

Deliberately built inland from the coast to escape the Berber raids, the streets of historic Benissa slope gently downhill. This tawny-coloured town, with its one long main street shaded with orange trees, seems a million miles from the razzmatazz of the big coastal resorts. Lovely old houses and mansions, the gable and porch designs clearly Moorish, and the windows protected by the traditional *rejas*, line streets such as Calle de la Purísima. The huge church of the Purísima, known as La Catedral de la Marina, dominates the central square. At the top of the town stands the peaceful Franciscan Convento de la Purísima, and there's an odd little Museo Etnológico (ethnographic museum) in the 15th-century agricultural exchange.

www.benissa.net

➕ 23G ✉ 26km (16 miles) north of Benidorm 🍴 Restaurants/bars (€–€€) 🚌 From Benidorm 🚆 From Benidorm ❓ Fira i Porrat di Sant Antoni (3 weeks in Jan)

ℹ️ Calle Francisco Sendra 2 ☎ 965 73 29 91

CABO DE LA NAO (CAP DE LA NAU)

The headland of Cabo de la Nao, the most easterly point on the Costa Blanca, soars above the sea to the south of Jávea (Xàbia). This stretch of coast makes a wonderful contrast to the flat sandy beaches to the north. Creamy white and ochre-tinted cliffs rise steeply from the sea below, the slopes clad in pines and sweet-smelling scrub vegetation. Unsurprisingly, the tourist boom attracted developers, and much of the surrounding area is dotted with secluded holiday villas. From the cape and its lighthouse there are superb views along the cliffs to the south and a road leads on to the lovely cove at Granadella (➤ 72). South of here there are no roads and experienced walkers can enjoy the unspoiled coast.

➕ 24G ✉ 50km (31 miles) north of Benidorm 🍴 Restaurant and bars (€–€€)

CABO DE SAN MARTÍN (CAP DE SANT MARTÍ)

The beautiful bay of Jávea is sheltered at its southern end by the Cabo de San Martín, a rocky promontory where it is easy to escape the crowds of the nearby beaches.

South of Jávea (Xàbia; ➤ 143) a path drops from the road at the Cruz de Portichol, a stone wayside cross from where both the cape and the island of Portichol (Isla de Portitxol) are visible. This leads out to San Martín, running through clumps of lavender, thyme and rosemary, to emerge at the headland. The all-round views are excellent; north to the town and beaches of Jávea, south to precipitous cliffs and the island. Other tracks lead up and down the coast, one to Cala Sardinera (➤ 72), a secluded little beach.

➕ 24G ✉ 50km (31 miles) north of Benidorm

CALPE (CALP)

The coast north of Benidorm has a chain of good beaches, classy villas hidden behind bougainvillaea-hung walls and relaxed family resorts. Calpe is one of the most popular of these, due mainly to the soaring mass of the Peñón de Ifach (► 48–49). This former fishing village, with its *mudéjar* church, towers, walls and museums (Museo Arqueológico and Museo Fester), has seen immense development since the mid-1990s, with soaring apartment blocks and hotels encroaching up the coast, and sprawling urbanizations climbing the hills behind the town. Its two splendid sandy beaches are often crowded in summer, but if you're looking for a buzzing resort with plenty of action that's smaller than Benidorm, try Calpe. Escape the hordes by taking a boat trip round the Peñón or a stroll near the salt flats behind town. Calpe has great shops, good sporting facilities, numerous restaurants and a lively summer nightlife.

www.calpe.es

✚ 22G ✉ 18km (11 miles) north of Benidorm

🍴 Restaurants/bars (€–€€€) 🚌 From Benidorm 🚢 Crucero por la Costa, Explanada del Puerto (☎ 965 85 00 52); Ifach Charter, Explanada del Puerto (☎ 965 84 55 35) ❓ See tourist office for festival information

ℹ Plaza del Mosquit s/n ☎ 965 83 85 32

COCENTAINA

The thriving inland town of Cocentaina in the Serpis valley is one of the most historic in the area, its medieval Christian and Arab quarters still clearly delineated below its ancient castle. Packed with fine old buildings and churches, the town is noted for its fiestas and superb local cooking. The major tourist attraction is the **Palau Comtal,** a magnificent, and recently restored, 13th- to 15th-century fortified palace. Its lovely rooms include the Sala Dorada and the Sala de Embajadores, with tiled Renaissance floors and exuberant baroque ceilings. The most notable church is the Mare Déu, and there are two museums, the Museu del Centre d'Estudis Contestans, featuring the whole story of Cocentaina with displays and an audiovisual programme, and the Casa Museu del Fester, devoted to the important Moros y Cristianos festival.

✚ 20K ✉ 60km (37 miles) west of Benidorm 🍽 Choice of restaurants and bars (€–€€€) 🚌 From Alicante ❓ Moros y Cristianos (8–11 Aug); Fira de Tots Sants (1 Nov) ℹ️ Palau Comtal, Plaza del Pla s/n ☎ 965 59 01 59

Palau Comtal
☎ 965 59 08 69
🕐 Mon–Sat 11–7
✋ Inexpensive

COLL DE RATES

The Coll de Rates road (➤ 146), less than 20 minutes' drive from Benidorm, is one of the most scenic on the Costa Blanca and gives a chance for a quick and easy taste of the beauty of the inland sierras. The road climbs and twists steadily through increasingly mountainous scenery to the pass, which lies at 780m (2,560ft). Driving from the north the rise is gradual, the fruit orchards and vegetable farms of the fertile agricultural plain dropping away and the vegetation changing as views of the sea emerge. Fruit and olive trees give way to almonds, while higher still, the hillsides support varied Mediterranean flora, seen at its best in the spring. Through the coll, the southern landscape is enclosed by the dramatic Parcent and Aixorta mountains.

✛ 22H ✉ 40km (25 miles) north of Benidorm 🍴 Choice of restaurants and bars en route (€–€€€)

DÉNIA

Lying beneath the heights of the Montgó natural park (➤ 46–47), historic and elegant Dénia is a far less brash holiday resort than some of its neighbours. Inhabited by the Phoenicians and the Greeks, it was named in honour of the Roman goddess Diana; the inhabitants are still known as *dianenses*. English raisin-dealers lived here throughout the 19th century and many are buried in the almost-forgotten English cemetery; the town's broad streets and solid buildings date from this time. A small Museo Etnológico has displays on the town's early history. Dénia's other attractions include the Castillo de Dénia (castle), perched high above the town and housing a small Museo Arqueológico (archaeological museum), the lovely 18th-century Church of the Assumption, and a picturesque old quarter near the fishing port. From here, ferries run to the Balearic Islands and a narrow-gauge train runs down the coast to Alicante (Alacant). But a car is probably the best way to see the lovely coastline to the south.

www.denia.net

✚ 24H ✉ 55km (34 miles) north of Benidorm 🍴 Choice of restaurants and bars (€–€€€) 🚌 From Benidorm ⛴ To Ibiza and Palma, Mallorca: Balearia Lines, Estación Marítima ☎ 902 16 01 80; www.balearia.com
ℹ Plaza Oculista Buigues 9 ☎ 966 42 23 67 🎇 Fallas de San José

(16–19 Mar), Romería a la Virgen de Rocío (Jun), Hogueras de San Juan (20–24 Jun), Fiesta de la Santísima Sangre (2nd Wed after 28 Jun), Moros y Cristianos y San Roque (14–16 Aug)

FUENTES DEL ALGAR (FONTS DE L'ALGAR)

Better known by their Valencian name – Fonts de l'Algar – the falls of the River Algar, which rises in the high sierras behind the Benidorm coast, are high on the list of major tourist honeypots. A series of crystal-clear cascades and falls has been landscaped and attracts countless visitors who enjoy the waterside paths and bathe in the pools and falls. The approach through the hills to this spot is beautiful; the road winds past loquat plantations, the main crop of the valley. The sight and sound of water on a hot summer day is enchanting, and the **Museo de Medio Ambiente** (environmental museum) and aromatic plant collection are added attractions.

✚ 21H ✉ 16km (10 miles) from Benidorm ☎ 965 88 21 06 🍴 Bars and restaurants nearby (€–€€)

Museo de Medio Ambiente
☎ 965 97 21 29 🕒 Daily 9–6
👋 Moderate

GALLINERA VALLEY

Best places to see,
➤ 40–41.

GANDÍA

Gandía, with more than 20km (12.5 miles) of clean golden sand, an elegant promenade and busy restaurants, promotes itself as a

beach resort (▶ 73). Tourism began here in the 1950s and many visitors never go near Gandía proper, a largely modern city on the River Serpis. It flourished in the 15th century, its wealth derived from sugar and silk. The main monuments date from this time. The star attraction is the Palacio de Santo Duque, a sumptuous 14th- to 17th-century pile built round a courtyard, its interior dripping with gold leaf; look out for the beautiful *azulejos* and Arab wall tiles. The collegiate church of Santa María is an austere and serene example of Catalan Gothic and the old medieval hospital now houses the town's archaeological museum.

www.abcgandia.com

✚ 23K ✉ 70km (43 miles) north of Benidorm 🍴 Choice of restaurants and bars (€–€€€) 🚌 From Benidorm ❓ See tourist office for festival information
ℹ Marqués de Campo s/n ☎ 962 87 77 88; Paseo Neptuno s/n ☎ 962 84 24 07

GORGOS VALLEY (VALL DE GORGOS)

The River Gorgos is joined by the river Castell west of the little town of Gata de Gorgos, and runs into the sea at Jávea (Xàbia, ▶ 143). The landscape of this gentle agricultural valley, surrounded by gradually rising hills, is known for its citrus groves and its vineyards. Here the traditional way of life has been untouched by the coastal tourist boom. Gata itself straddles the main road, but the peaceful old town makes a good stop, especially if you're interested in cane and rattan ware. Cane and esparto grass have been used here for centuries to make the matting and furniture still on sale today, though much is now imported. West from Gata, orange groves start to give way to vineyards. The traditional grape here is the *moscatello*, used in the production of wines of the same name, still a speciality of Alicante (Alacant) province. The raisins made from these grapes were famed in the 19th century, when they were shipped from Dénia (➤ 138–139). The attractive old houses, now largely uninhabited, are called *ríu-raus*; their arched porches were designed for drying the grapes. Jalón (Xaló) lies surrounded by this fertile land, a tranquil town with a striking church and local wine for sale in its shops. From here the valley narrows, the sierras rise on either side, and the villages become more scattered.

✚ 23G ✉ 30km (18.5 miles), northwest of Benidorm 🍴 Choice of restaurants and bars (€–€€€)

GUADALEST
Best places to see, ➤ 42–43.

GUADALEST VALLEY (VALL DE GUADALEST)

Most visitors to the Costa Blanca make the trip to the castle at
Guadalest (➤ 42–43), but few explore further into the valley, one
of the most beautiful in the province. Blessed by the Guadalest
river and abundant springs, it was first terraced and irrigated by the
Moors, and is sheltered on all sides by high mountains and
dramatic peaks. These create a micro-climate ideal for
the wide range of fruit trees that have been grown
here for centuries. The oranges and loquats of the
lower slopes give way to almonds as the road climbs;
in early spring the entire hillside is a sea of pink
blossom. Olive trees gradually appear to replace the
almonds, only to give way to pine and mountain
shrubs as the road reaches its highest point at the
Puerto de Ares, from where another valley system
opens out towards Alcoy (Alcoi; ➤ 130–131). Among
the white villages strung along the valley road
(➤ 64–65) are Benifato, Benimantell, Beniardá and Confrides.
Stop in them to wander quaint streets, hung with bougainvillaea
and geraniums, and absorb the grandeur of encircling mountains.

🗺 21J ✉ 15km (9 miles) north of Benidorm 🍴 Choice of restaurants and
bars (€–€€€) 🚌 From Benidorm ❓ Fiestas in Benimantell, Beniardá,
Benifato and Confrides

JÁVEA (XÀBIA)

Jávea, today known mainly as a friendly and fun family resort, had a long and respectable history before its spread down the hill towards the beautiful and protected beaches. Believed to be the sunniest place on the coast, the town lies on a bay embraced by the promontories of Cabo de San Antonio (Cap de Sant Antoni; ➤ 46–47) to the north and pine-studded Cabo de la Nao (Cap de la Nau; ➤ 134) to the south. The narrow streets of the old town are lined with handsome houses, ornamented with delicate stonework and wrought-iron *rejas* and balconies. Fine buildings cluster around the Plaza de la Iglesia, with its fortified Gothic church of San Bartolomé and dignified town hall.

Just down the street the local Museo Arqueológico, Histórico y Etnográfico (archaeological, historical and ethnographic museum) is housed in a Gothic palace; it traces Jávea's history from Iberian and Roman times to the emergence of the Christian kingdoms, and gives pride of place to replicas of exquisite Iberian gold jewellery found nearby. The port area, called the Aduanas de Mar, has a busy working harbour. Here you'll find the fish market and fishing boats, the modern church of Nuestra Señora de Loreto with its roof like a ship's hull, long stretches of safe beach and shops, bars and restaurants. Jávea, with its good facilities, friendly atmosphere, and easy access to the unspoiled country of Montgó (➤ 46–47) is a popular base for holiday-makers of all ages.

www.xabia.org

✚ 24G ✉ 55km (34 miles) north of Benidorm 🍴 Choice of restaurants and bars (€–€€€) 🚌 From Benidorm ❓ Fogueras de Sant Joan (24 Jun), Moros y Cristianos (last weekend in Jul), Nuestra Señora de Loreto (1–8 Sep)
ℹ Jávea: Carrer Almirante Bastarreche 11, Aduanas de Mar ☎ 965 79 07 36; Plaza de la Iglesia 6 ☎ 965 79 43 56

MONTGÓ AND CABO DE SAN ANTONIO
Best places to see, ➤ 46–47.

MORAIRA
As much an area as a village, Moraira's name for many people is synonymous with expensive second homes and resident expatriates. Originally a fishing village on a sheltered bay below a rocky headland, Moraira lies well off the main coast road and is undisturbed by the sort of crowds that flock to the main resorts. Many spacious villas are scattered among the pine woods that run down to the sea, but with only a handful of hotels, Moraira remains one of the most unspoiled resorts, with a variety of services aimed specifically at its foreign residents. A lovely coastline, a superbly restored 18th-century castle, good sports facilities, upmarket shops and one of Spain's best restaurants, Girasol (➤ 156), all tempt visitors to return.

➕ 23G ✉ 35km (22 miles) from Benidorm 🍴 Choice of restaurants and bars (€–€€€)

ℹ️ Carretera Moraira-Teulada 51 ☎ 965 74 51 68

OLIVA

North of Jávea (Xàbia) the coastline is flatter, becoming an almost continuous strip of smooth sandy beaches, ideal for small children and their families. The coastal towns and resorts cater efficiently for large numbers of summer visitors, with hotels, restaurants, sports facilities, marinas, entertainment and shops. Playa de Oliva is one of these, but inland lies the old town, once part of a dukedom founded in 1449 by Alfonso el Magnánimo, with the remnants of the old ducal castle to be found outside the town. The surrounding flat, fertile ground, now planted with oranges, was originally marshland, and some wetlands remain. The old town centre has some fine 16th-century buildings and the wonderfully higgledy-piggledy white-washed quarter of Santa Ana.

✚ 23J ✉ 42km (26 miles) north of Benidorm

🍴 Choice of restaurants and bars (€–€€€)

🛈 Passeig Lluís Vivès s/n ☎ 962 85 55 28

a drive from Pego to La Nucia

Start at Pego (southwest of Oliva) and leave the town by the C3318 (715) heading southeast to the hills of the Sierra de Alfaro and the Sierra de Aixorta.

Once surrounded by rice fields, the lively town of Pego feels a long way from the coastal resorts. It still retains its wide town gates and the parish church has a lovely 15th-century altarpiece depicting the pregnant Madonna.

The route follows the C3318 (715) to Orba. Leave the town and follow the road into the hills towards the Coll de Rates pass (➤ 137).

As the road climbs, superb views open out towards the coast: villages and hamlets scattered across the plain, a

patchwork of fields and ever-widening glimpses of the sea and the coastal massifs. There are several points where you can admire the views.

Once over the pass continue on the C3318 (715) all the way to Polop (▶ 148) and La Nucia.

Over the pass the scenery becomes more breathtaking as the road descends towards the Guadalest valley and the Fuentes del Algar (Fonts de l'Algar, ▶ 139). Terraces are planted with almonds, loquats and oranges and the dramatic crags of Aixorta rise up to the south. La Nucia is worth a stop, particularly on a Sunday when it hosts a large street market.

Distance 55km (34 miles)
Time 2 hours without stops, all day with visits and shopping
Start point Pego ✚ 23J
End point La Nucia ✚ 21H (near Polop)
Lunch Ca L'Angeles (€€) ✉ Gabriel Miró 16, Polop ☎ 965 87 02 26

PEÑÓN DE IFACH
Best places to see, ➤ 48–49.

POLOP
Few visitors bother to stop at Polop, a foothill town on the Guadalest road, but this small white-washed *pueblo* is well worth the easy trip from Benidorm. A visit here is a chance to see an everyday inland town, largely untouched by the development seen on the coast. Lovely old buildings line the narrow streets, the church is a fine example of local architecture, and a ruined castle and a clutch of good restaurants complete the picture. The main attraction is the Font Els Xorros, an ancient fountain with 221 spouts which has been renovated, but the Museo del Alambre, with its medieval basement, is also worth a quick visit. Polop has always been noted for its craftwork, and lace, embroidery and woollen goods in traditional styles and patterns are still made locally.

➕ 21H ✉ 12km (7.5 miles) north of Benidorm 🍴 Choice of restaurants and bars (€–€€€) 🚌 From Benidorm ❓ San Roque (15 Aug), San Francisco de Borja (4 Oct)

ℹ Polop de la Marina: Carretera Benidorm, Polop Esq G Miró-Teulería
☎ 966 89 60 72

SIERRA DE AITANA (SERRA D'AITANA)
When the coast is sweltering in the summer heat, it's tempting to head for the hills. Easily accessible from Alicante (Alacant) and Benidorm, the Sierra de Aitana makes a good choice, with attractions for all the family, breathtaking mountain scenery, fresh breezes and cooler temperatures. The range takes its name from the

peak of Aitana, at 1,558m (5,111ft) the highest summit in the Costa Blanca's northern sierras. You can drive nearly to the top and there are wonderful views over woodland to the surrounding mountains and the coast. Excellent hiking country, the Sierra has good trails and paths and picnic areas for families; children will enjoy the area's safari park (➤ 71).

On the edge of the mountains, the pretty villages of Sella and Alcolecha (Alcoleja) are worth a visit; both have good restaurants.

✚ 21J ✉ 30km (18.5 miles) west of Benidorm 🍴 Restaurants and bars (€–€€€)

SIERRA HELADA

Benidorm is sheltered to the north by the Sierra Helada, the ice hills, a mountainous promontory so-called for its lower temperatures and the optical effect of moonlight on its rocky slopes. Riddled with caves used by the Iberians, the headland was mined by the Phoenicians and Romans, and two watchtowers bear witness to its role as a look-out point during the 17th-century pirate raids. The 21st century has left the Sierra untouched, and within a ten-minute bus ride from downtown Benidorm you can find beautiful hill walks. Tracks lead out to the headlands of Punta de la Escaleta and the lighthouse at Punta Bombarda, while a magnificent path runs along the crest of the ridge, overlooking the sea and coastline.
www.benidorm.org

⊞ 21G ⊠ 2km (1.2 miles) north of Benidorm ¶¶ None ⊟ From Benidorm
ℹ Benidorm: Avenida Martínez Alejos 16 ☎ 965 85 32 24

VILLAJOYOSA (LA VILA JOIOSA)

Ancient Villajoyosa, 'the jewelled town', with its Roman and Moorish origins, started modern life as a fishing village, protected by encircling walls and huddled round its massive and beautiful Gothic church. The old quarter, with its brightly coloured houses in blue and green and ochre, is still the heart of what has become a popular holiday town, with a long sandy beach and everything for the modern visitor, including the **Museo Etnográfico**

(ethnographic museum), a **chocolate musem** and the Costa Blanca's main casino. Villajoyosa is at its most exuberant in July, when the week-long Moros y Cristianos festival takes place, one of the region's most rumbustious. Splendidly costumed as Moors,

Christians, pirates and slave-girls, locals re-enact key events, including the sacking of the town's castle by the dastardly pirate Zala Arráez in 1538.

✠ 20H ✉ 10km (6 miles) south of Benidorm 🍴 Choice of restaurants and bars (€–€€€) 🚌 From Benidorm 🚆 From Benidorm ❓ Virgen del Carmen

(15–16 Jul), Moros y Cristianos (24–31 Jul)

ℹ Avenida País Valencià 10 ☎ 966 85 13 71

Museo Etnográfico

✉ Barranquet 16 ☎ 965 89 01 50; www.museusdelavilajoiosa.com ⏰ Mon–Fri 10–1:30, 5–7, Sat 10–1:30 ✋ Inexpensive

Museo del Chocolate

✉ Avenida Pianista Gonzalo Soriano 13 ☎ 965 89 09 50; www.valor.es ⏰ Mon–Fri 9:30–12:30, 3:30–5:30 ✋ Free

HOTELS

BENIDORM

Agir (€€€)

A long-established hotel on Benidorm's main avenue, with luxurious, creatively designed rooms.

✉ Avenida Mediterráneo 11 ☎ 965 85 51 62; www.hotelagir.com

Cimbel (€€€)

One of Benidorm's most traditional hotels, right next to the Playa de Levante, with a pool and air-conditioning.

✉ Avenida Europa 1 ☎ 965 85 21 00; www.hotelcimbel.com

Dynastic (€€€)

Super modern hotel situated near Levante beach, with panoramic lifts affording magnificent views. All the amenities, with pleasant rooms, a choice of pools, café-bars and an impressive spa.

✉ L'Ametila del Mar 15 ☎ 965 85 36 00; www.hoteldynastic.com

Gran Hotel Bali (€€€)

Towering over Benidorm's already impressively high skyline, the Gran Hotel Bali has made its mark as Europe's tallest hotel. The majority of rooms have a balcony or terrace, and there are three outdoor swimming pools.

✉ Luis Prendes s/n ☎ 965 85 42 43; www.granhotelbali.com

Sol Pelicanos (€€€)

Four pools, tennis courts and close to beach; ideal for families looking for style and comfort. All rooms have bathrooms and balconies; entertainment for all ages.

✉ Gerona 45–47 ☎ 965 85 23 50; www.solmelia.com

CALPE (CALP)

Galetamar (€€)

Modern, well-equipped hotel with balconies, sea views, good-size pool and spacious lounge areas. Accommodation includes family rooms and individual bungalows.

✉ La Caleta 28 ☎ 965 83 23 11; www.galetamar.com

COCENTAINA
Els Frares (€€)
A tiny hotel well outside town in an elegantly restored old house, located in a mountain village with wonderful views.
✉ Avenida del País Valencia, Quatretondeta ☎ 965 51 12 34; www.inn-spain.com

DÉNIA
Buenavista (€€€)
Surrounded by pine trees, this small and lovely hotel, with pool, is housed in a skilfully converted 19th-century mansion.
✉ Partida Tossalet 82 ☎ 965 78 79 95; www.buenavistadenia.com

GANDÍA
Bayren 1 (€€)
A classic seaside hotel on the beach front, with all facilities and within a short walk's distance of all the resort's major attractions.
✉ Paseo Neptuno 62 ☎ 962 84 03 00

GUADALEST
El Trestellador (€)
A small family-run mountain hotel high in the Guadalest valley. Simple comfortable rooms, fine views and excellent local cooking.
✉ Partida del Trestellador, Benimantell ☎ 965 88 52 21

JÁTIVA (XÀTIVA)
Hostería de Mont Sant (€€€)
An elegant and historic country house hotel in a wonderful situation on the hillside above the town and below the castle. Lovely gardens, pool, superb views and the service is friendly.
✉ Carretera del Castillo s/n ☎ 962 27 50 81

JÁVEA (XÀBIA)
Parador de Jávea (€€€)
The only *parador* on the Costa Blanca, the de Jávea is a modern, luxury hotel beautifully situated in verdant gardens.
✉ Mediterráneo 233 ☎ 965 79 02 00; www.parador.es

MORAIRA
Swiss Moraira (€€€)

A relatively small hotel set back from the sea in a beautiful valley. There is a high level of comfort and ambience of tranquillity. All the facilities you would expect to find, including a swimming pool and tennis court.

✉ Haya 175, Urbanizacíon Club Moraira ☎ 965 74 71 04

VILLAJOYOSA (LA VILA JOIOSA)
El Montíboli (€€€)

This luxury hotel is set on a promontory high above two secluded bays and backed by hills. The hotel is also renowned for its superb restaurants.

✉ Partida Montíboli s/n ☎ 965 89 02 50; www.elmontiboli.com

RESTAURANTS

BENIDORM
L'Albufera (€)
See page 76.

La Palmera-Casa Paco Nadal (€€)

One of Benidorm's oldest restaurants, with a pretty terrace, specializing in fish and rice dishes.

✉ Avenida Dr Severo Ochoa 44, Rincón de Loix ☎ 965 85 32 82 ③ Lunch only except Jul–Aug. Closed Mon

Tapas del Mundo (€)
See page 77.

Rías Baixas (€€)

Grab a terrace table and sample plain grilled fish, excellent shell-fish and a selection of more international dishes at excellent value.

✉ Plaza Torrechó 3 ☎ 965 85 50 22 ③ Lunch and dinner. Closed Wed

ALTEA
El Patio (€€)
Specialities at this good local eatery include *paella, fideuà, arroz a la banda* and the freshest of plain grilled fish.

✉ Avenida del Puerto 9 ☎ 965 84 39 89 🕔 Lunch and dinner. Closed Thu and Nov–Feb

Sant Pere 24 (€€)
See page 59.

CALPE (CALP)
Baydal (€€)
This bustling restaurant by the port is the place for a great *paella*.

✉ Avenida del Puerto 12 ☎ 965 83 11 11 🕔 Lunch and dinner. Closed Mon Nov–Apr

DÉNIA
El Pegolí (€€)
See pages 58–59.

El Raset (€€€)
One of Dénia's oldest and best restaurants, in the old fishing quarter.

✉ Bellaviata 7 ☎ 965 78 50 40 🕔 Lunch and dinner

GANDÍA
Emilio (€€)
Sophisticated restaurant near the beach. Great use is made of fresh market produce; it makes a good choice for something a bit special.

✉ B Bloque F-5, Avenida Vicente Calderón 5 ☎ 962 84 07 61 🕔 Lunch and dinner. Closed Wed except Jul and Aug

GUADALEST
L'Obrer (€€)
See page 58.

JÁTIVA (XÀTIVA)
Casa la Abuela (€€€)
Excellent restaurant offering local recipes; look out for *arnadí*, a rich dessert cake made with pumpkin, almonds and pine-nuts.
✉ Reina 17 ☎ 962 28 10 85 🕓 Lunch and dinner. Closed Sun, and mid-Jun to mid-Aug

JÁVEA (XÀBIA)
Cabo la Nau (€€)
See pages 76–77.

Tasca Tonis (€)
The locals' favourite, so it's busy year-round. Home-cooking at its best, using local ingredients. There's a different 'special' every day.
✉ Mayor 2 ☎ 966 46 18 51 🕓 Lunch and dinner. Closed Sun pm

MORAIRA
Girasol (€€€)
A pretty chalet with a terrace considered the foremost restaurant in the region and one of the best in Spain.
✉ Carretera Moraira–Calpe Km 1.5 ☎ 965 74 43 73 🕓 Lunch and dinner (summer pm only except Sun). Closed Mon

POLOP
Ca L'Angeles (€€)
See page 58.

SHOPPING

ARTS, CRAFTS AND GIFTS
Ceramica les Sorts
Colourful pottery from the region – everything from jugs to gnomes.
✉ Carretera Moraira–Calpe, Edif Kristal Mar 18D–18E, Moraira
☎ 965 74 57 37

Cerámicas Valles
Vibrant, hand-painted ceramics; also leather and garden pots.
✉ Urb. Los Piños D-5, Ctra Calpe-Moraira Km 2, Calpe ☎ 965 833 661

BOOKS
Librería Inglesa
Good selection of new and second-hand English books, also titles in French, German and other European languages.
✉ Avenida Almería ☎ 965 85 08 11

FASHION, LEATHER AND JEWELLERY
Arpel
This well-stocked shop carries a good range of bags, purses, belts and other leather goods to cater for all tastes
✉ Calle Gambo 4, Benidorm ☎ 965 85 35 68

Bolsos Paco
Deliciously soft bags, travel goods, belts, wallets and purses.
✉ Mayor 35, Dénia ☎ 965 75 68 73

Goya Oro
Chic jeweller selling top-name watches and elegant jewellery in platinum, gold and silver.
✉ Martínez Alejos 3, Benidorm ☎ 966 83 10 50

Pecas Calzados
The two branches of this popular shoe shop.
✉ La Cruz 6 ☎ 962 87 73 16 ✉ Mayor 60, Gandía ☎ 962 87 81 03

Ritual
Pure cotton and silk clothing from India and the Far East.
✉ Marques de Campo 26, Dénia ☎ 966 43 01 19

Saqueta
Soft leather bags, purses and wallets.
✉ Mayor 17, Gandía ☎ 962 87 25 89

FOOD AND DRINK
La Boutique del Vino
A wide range of Spanish and foreign wines, spirits and liqueurs.
✉ Avda Atmella de Mar s/n, Benidorm ☎ 966 80 32 09

Especialities Lloret
This trendy food shop is a real boon for self-caterers and there is also a good range of tempting edible souvenirs.
✉ Juan Carlos I-3, Villajoyosa (La Vila Joiosa) ☎ 965 89 03 93

L'Alteana
Sumptuous calorie-heavy bread and cakes as well as an interesting range of savoury mouthfuls.
✉ Avenida de la Nucia 13, Altea ☎ 965 84 03 07

Sanct Bernhard
An interesting herbalist, worth visiting for its range of products that includes teas, creams and cleansers.
✉ Avenida Gabriel Miró 7, Calpe (Calp) ☎ 965 83 68 07

ENTERTAINMENT

BARS, NIGHTCLUBS AND SHOWS

Benidorm Palace
Popular international floorshow and cabaret with optional dinner.
✉ Avenida Dr Severo Ochoa s/n, Benidorm ☎ 965 85 16 60

Castillo Fortaleza de Alfaz
The castle offers a night out at a mock medieval banquet followed by a visit to a chamber of horrors and a futuristic disco.
✉ Carretera Benidorm–Albir, Benidorm ☎ 966 86 55 92

Imperial
Action-packed disco featuring the latest music and dance.
✉ Carretera Jávea, Dénia ☎ None 🕐 Daily 10:30pm–5am, Easter–Oct

KM
KM has a long-standing reputation for music and beautiful people.
✉ Levante Promenade, Benidorm ☎ None 🕐 Daily 11pm–6am, Easter–Oct

Molino Benidorm
Amusing floorshow followed by male striptease.
✉ Avenida Beniardá 2, Benidorm ☎ 966 80 23 08

Penélope

This huge, noisy and hip disco has been popular with Benidorm regulars for years.

✉ Antigua Ctra N-322, Benidorm ☎ None 🕐 Daily 11pm–6am

La Plaza

Live jazz on Friday nights.

✉ Plaza de la Inglesia, Altea ☎ None

CASINO
Casino Costa Blanca

✉ Carretera Nacional 332 (Valencia–Alicante Km 114.8, Villajoyosa (La Vila Joiosa) ☎ 965 89 07 00; www.casinomediterraneo.es 🕐 8pm–4am (5am Fri and Sat)

THEATRE AND CONCERTS
Amphitheatres

Programme of concerts, ballets and plays performed in July and August by international and Spanish groups and singers.

✉ Aiguera Park, Benidorm

Palau Altea

A full programme of music, theatre and dance.

✉ Palau Altea, Casc Antic, Altea ☎ 966 88 19 24; www.palaualtea.com

SPORT

BOWLING
Bowling Centre Benidorm

✉ Avenida Mediterráneo 22, Benidorm ☎ 965 85 41 87

GOLF
Club de Golf Don Cayo

✉ Urbanización El Aramo–Sierra de Altea, Calpe (Calp) ☎ 965 84 80 46

Club de Golf Ifach

✉ Carretera Moraira–Calpe Km 3, Urbanización San Jaime, Moraira ☎ 966 49 71 14

Club de Golf Jávea
✉ Carretera Jávea–Benitatxell Km 4.5, Jávea (Xàbia) ☎ 965 79 25 84

Club de Golf La Sella
✉ Carretera La Xara–Jesús Pobre, Dénia ☎ 966 45 42 52

HORSE-RIDING
Rancho Sierra Helada
✉ Sierra Helada, Benidorm ☎ 678 98 31 19

SAILING
Club Náutico Dénia
✉ Carretera Dénia–Jávea 1, Dénia ☎ 965 78 09 89

Club Náutico Moraira
✉ Puerto de Moraira ☎ 965 74 44 61

SCUBA DIVING
Aquatic Dénia
✉ Carretera Dénia–Jávea 3d, Les Rotes, Dénia ☎ 966 42 52 15

Club Poseidon
✉ Santander 9, Alfaz 4, Edif Silvia, Benidorm ☎ 966 80 17 84

España Bajo el Mar
✉ Puerto Blanco, Calpe (Calp) ☎ 965 83 13 37

Scuba Diving Benidorm
✉ Avenida Otto de Habsburgo 10, Benidorm ☎ 966 80 97 12

WATERSKIING AND WINDSURFING
Cable Ski
✉ Racó de L'Oix, Playa de Levante, Benidorm ☎ 965 85 13 86

Marco Polo Expediciones
✉ Avenida Europa 5, Benidorm ☎ 965 86 33 99; www.marco-polo-exp.es

Murcia

The province of Murcia lies south of Alicante (Alacant) and stretches inland to Albacete and southwards to Almería. Known since Moorish times for the fertility of its land, Murcia's agriculture has prospered as its once-rich mines have declined. Much of the province is planted with fruit, olives, rice, nuts and vegetables, particularly around its capital, Murcia.

Murcia

Inland lie arid and beautiful mountain ranges, vineyards, historic towns and forgotten villages, where few tourists venture. The coastline has a wide variety of scenery, from the shallow waters and flat landscapes of the Mar Menor to the secret coves and empty beaches around Mazarrón. This area is popular with Spaniards, particularly around the Mar Menor, which has the best facilities of Murcia's resorts. From a base here, excursions are possible through undeveloped and little-explored valleys, and superb mountain scenery, to hill towns such as Jumilla and Mula.

MURCIA

Founded on the Segura river in the 9th century by the Moors, the city of Murcia soon became an important trading centre, its wealth largely based on the fertility of the outlying *huerta* (market gardens). By the 1300s it was the regional capital and continued to prosper, its 18th-century wealth funding the majority of its finest buildings. Today, it's an agricultural and commercial centre, a delightful and truly Spanish city which makes few concessions to tourism.

It's worth battling through the modern suburbs to spend time

in the historic centre, a largely pedestrianized maze of narrow streets and squares, punctuated by elegant buildings and churches. The major sights, including the magnificent baroque cathedral (➤ 52–53), cluster around the medieval arteries of the Trapería and Platería, today trendy shopping streets. Here you'll find the bizarre 19th-century Casino (➤ 163), the Teatro Romea, and a clutch of superb churches. Other fine buildings line the river, where there are shady walkways and peaceful green gardens. Murcia is well endowed with museums; the **Museo Arqueológico Provincial** (archaeological museum) traces the area's history and the Museo Salzillo (Salzillo Museum; ➤ 164–165) celebrates the woodcarving genius of one of its natives. Local pride in traditional artisan work and craftsmanship is evident at the **Centro Regional de Artesanía.**
www.murciaturistica.es

➕ 7E ❓ Semana Santa (Mar/Apr), Spring Festival (week after Easter), Entierra de la Sardina (Easter week)

ℹ Plaza Cardenal Belluga s/n ☎ 902 10 10 70; Plano de San Francisco s/n ☎ 968 35 87 20 and 968 35 87 49

Museo Arqueológico Provincial

✉ Gran Vía Alfonso X el Sablo 5 ☎ 968 23 46 02 🕐 Jul–Aug Mon–Sat 9–2, Sun 10–2; Sep–Jun Mon–Fri 10–2, 6–8, Sat–Sun 11–2 💰 Moderate

Centro Regional de Artesanía

✉ Francisco Rabal 6 ☎ 968 35 75 37 🕐 Mon–Sat 11–2, 5:30–8:30, Sun 12–2

Casino

Built between 1847 and 1901, this memorable structure, still in use today, was once the town's main social meeting place, offering members a library, meeting rooms, billiard room and ballroom. An eclectic stylistic mixture of Moorish features, marble and metalwork, French-inspired grandeur, painted ceilings and English craftsmanship, the Casino is high on a must-see list. From the Moorish vestibule a central gallery leads to the library, designed by an English firm and exuding Edwardian rectitude.

In stark contrast, the ballroom opposite, with its musicians' gallery, vast painted ceiling and dazzling chandeliers evokes the style of old Vienna, while the high point for most visitors is the ladies' powder room, a neo-baroque fantasy with a fine painted ceiling and huge decorative gilt mirrors.

🚩 *Murcia 4b*

✉ Calle Trapería 22

☎ 968 21 22 55

🕐 Currently closed for restoration; phone for latest information

🍴 Bars and restaurants nearby (€–€€€) 🎟 Free

Catedral de Santa María
Best places to see, ➤ 52–53.

Churches
If you're interested in ecclesiastical architecture, Murcia is full of delights, and fans of the baroque will find many staggering examples of this dramatic and exuberant style. Among the best churches are La Merced, San Miguel, Santa Ana and Santa Clara, grouped together on the edge of the old town, and all with superb façades and Salzillo carvings inside. Another good trio is San Pedro, San Nicolás and Santa Catalina in the same area of town.

✚ *Murcia 4c, 3c, 4c, 3c, 3b, 3b, 3b* respectively 🕓 Daily 9–1, 5–7 ✋ Free

Museo de Bellas Artes
A large and variable collection of pictures giving a comprehensive view of the development of Murcian painting from the 15th to the 20th centuries.

✚ *Murcia 5c* ✉ Obispo Frutos 8 ☎ 968 23 93 46 🕓 Tue–Sat 10–8:30, Sun 10–2 ✋ Moderate

Museo de la Catedral
Housed in the cloister of Murcia's great cathedral (➤ 52–53), this museum houses early sculpture, including a Roman sarcophagus, and gives pride of place to the huge and ornate 600kg (1,320-pound) gold and silver monstrance, used at the feast of Corpus Christi.

✚ *Murcia 4b* (in cathedral) ✉ Plaza de la Cruz 2 ☎ 968 21 63 44 🕓 Apr–Sep daily 10–1, 5–8; Oct–Mar daily 10–1, 5–7 ✋ Inexpensive

Museo Salzillo
This is probably Murcia's most important museum, displaying a huge collection of work by the 18th-century wood sculptor Francisco Salzillo, born in Murcia. He specialized in dramatic and detailed polychrome figures and scenes from the life of Christ.

Most of these were designed to be carried through the streets during the Holy Week processions, as indeed they are still. The Nativity scene, with over 500 rustic figures, is worth a close look.
➕ *Murcia 2c* ✉ Plaza San Agustín 3 ☎ 968 29 18 93 🕐 Currently closed for restoration; phone for latest information ✋ Moderate

San Juan de Dios
The oval interior of this flamboyant baroque building has doubled up as both church and museum for some years. The usual Catholic Mass is celebrated every Sunday, but for the rest of the week the church acts as an elegant ecclesiastical backdrop for a fine collection of religious imagery, including works by artists such as Salzillo, Beltrán and Bussy.
➕ *Murcia 4b* ✉ Eulogio Soriano 4 ☎ 968 21 45 41 🕐 Tue–Sat 10–2, 5–8:30, Sun 10–2 ✋ Free

a walk around central Murcia

Start at Plaza de Santo Domingo, a large square with bars and flower stalls, dominated by a magnificent fig tree, and head down pedestrianized Calle Trapería, one of the city's smartest shopping streets.

The Casino (➤ 163) is a short way down on the left. The street opens up into Plaza Hermádez Amores, with the great tower and north façade of the cathedral (➤ 52–53) in front of you. Cut right down Calle Escultor Salzillo to Plaza Cardinal Belluga, adorned with orange trees, where the cathedral's main façade provides a contrast to the sober Renaissance front of the Bishop's Palace to your right.

Take Calle Arenal, down the side of the palace, south towards the river and the peaceful terrace of the Glorieta

España. From here turn right on to Gran Vía Francisco Salzillo, a busy modern boulevard lined with shops. Turn right along Calle Santa Catalina to Plaza de San Bartolome, with its church of the same name. Turn left into little Plaza Jose Esteve Mora, then right into Calle Platería then left, soon after, along Calle Alfaro,

to emerge opposite the pale pink 19th-century Teatro Romea. Take tiny Calle Arco de Santo Domingo and pass under the arch to arrive back at your starting point.

Distance 1.5km (1 mile)
Time 2–3 hours, depending on visits
Start/end point Plaza de Santo Domingo ✚ *Murcia 4c* 🚌 3, 4
Lunch Mesón el Corral (€€) ✉ Plaza de Santo Domingo 23–24
☎ 968 21 45 97

More to see in Murcia

ÁGUILAS

Well off most foreigners' routes, Águilas is one of the most southerly of the resorts in this area, lying on the Golfo de Mazarrón. This arid stretch of coast is a popular Spanish holiday area that has kept much of its character, and escaped the worst development. First inhabited by the Phoenicians, followed by the Romans and Arabs, Águilas's modern appearance dates largely from the 1780s when the present grid-patterned town was built to serve as a port for the local mines. The older fishing quarter, overlooked by the castle of San Juan and the Cope watchtower, still survives; Águilas is still an important port with a daily market. A fine British-built locomotive near the seafront commemorates the importance of the railway in Águilas's economic heyday. Two excellent beaches and a string of virtually undiscovered coves lie on either side of the town, making it a good base if you're looking for a tranquil beach holiday.

www.aguilas.org

⊞ 1D ⊠ 80km (49 miles) southeast of Murcia ⛊ Choice of restaurants and bars (€–€€€) 🚌 From Murcia 🚊 From Murcia ⓘ Plaza Antonio Cortijo s/n ☎ 968 49 32 85

ALEDO

The little town of Aledo, situated on the lower slopes of the Sierra de Espuña (➤ 54–55) and founded as a Moorish stronghold, was once an important frontier town, held from the 13th to the 15th centuries by the Order of Santiago. Today it's a good example of a thriving Murcian country town and a good stopping point if you're driving, its narrow white streets giving glimpses of the fabulous view towards the coast. Just outside is the **Ermita de Santa Eulalia** (open dawn–dusk), a lovely little building with an exquisite *mudéjar* ceiling and frescoes telling the story of the eponymous saint, hounded to death by Roman soldiers.

⊞ 4F ⊠ 43km (27 miles) south of Murcia ⛊ Choice of restaurants and bars (€–€€)

CALBLANQUE

Best places to see, ➤ 36–37.

CARTAGENA

Cartagena, built around a superb natural harbour, was founded by Hannibal as his Iberian capital and named after North African Carthage. A Roman port and administrative centre, its strategic importance continued for centuries, as the numerous surrounding castles and the vast Arsenal testify. Its wealth came from mining, which paid for churches such as Santa Maria de Gracia and La Caridad, as well as the large number of Modernist buildings around the city. Today, the first impression is of a rather run-down industrial city with a naval dockyard and extensive modern suburbs. It's worth persevering, however, as the old city has some of Murcia's best museums, superb architecture, atmospheric streets and old-fashioned shops.

There's a fine view of the harbour and city layout from Parque Torres, from where the road winds back down to the main plaza past the ruined Catedral Vieja, thought to be one of Spain's oldest churches. A palm-lined esplanade runs beside

the port to Isaac Perel's submarine, a world-first, built here in 1888. Down in the old town is the church of Santa Maria, with a wonderful collection of carved wooden figures, used in Cartagena's Holy Week processions. Look out particularly for the Gran Hotel, the Casa Cervantes and Llagostera, all fine Modernist buildings.

Museums worth visiting are the **Museo Arqueológico Municipal,** which has a large Roman collection, and the **Museo Nacional de Arqueología Marítima,** with many underwater shipwreck finds.

www.ayto-cartagena.es

✚ 5B ✉ 53km (33 miles) southeast of Murcia 🍴 Choice of restaurants and bars (€–€€€) 🚌 From Murcia 🚆 From Murcia ❓ Carnaval (Feb/Mar), Semana Santa (Mar/Apr), Cartagineses y Romanos (24–30 Sep)

ℹ Puertas de San José, Plaza Almirante Bastarreche s/n ☎ 968 50 64 83

Museo Arqueológico Municipal

✉ Ramón y Cajal 45 ☎ 968 53 90 27 🕐 Tue–Fri 10–2, 5–8, Sat–Sun 11–2 ✋ Free

Museo Nacional de Arqueología Marítima

✉ Dique de Navidad s/n ☎ 968 12 11 66 🕐 Tue–Sun 10–3 ✋ Free

❓ Scheduled to move to Muelle de Alfonso XII during 2008

FORTUNA

A few kilometres outside the workaday town of Fortuna lies the Balneario, one of Murcia's handful of thermal hot springs. Used by the Romans and Arabs, the water quality is among the best in Europe for rheumatic and respiratory complaints. The spa's layout today dates from the late 19th century, with dignified hotels set around palm-shaded promenades. Deep below lies the spring, gushing out at a temperature of 53°C (127°F), channelled directly into the treatment rooms. Here you can wallow in a marble bath or enjoy a range of showers and massages. If this sounds daunting, there are plenty of other facilities, including a steaming open-air swimming pool fed by the springs.

➕ 9F ✉ 22km (13.5 miles) north of Murcia 🕔 Baths and treatments: daily 8–1; swimming pool: 10–9 ☎ 968 68 50 11 🖐 Moderate 🍴 Restaurant and bar (€–€€) 🚌 From Murcia 🚃 From Murcia

ℹ Avenida Juan Carlos I s/n ☎ 968 68 55 86

JUMILLA

Set in the rolling sierras of Murcia's northern corner, Jumilla, a small agricultural and market town well off the beaten track, is a mecca for wine buffs. First planted by the Romans, the vineyards are among Europe's oldest and some of the very few not to have been damaged by the 19th-century phylloxera outbreak. The full-bodied and intense reds have an alcohol content as high as 16 per cent – best drunk mature, the mid-1980s are the years to look out for. You can learn more in the idiosyncratic **Museo del**

Vino Juan Carcelén (wine museum) before a visit to the lovely Franciscan monastery and its little museum, the **Museo Municipal Jerónimo Molina.** Other high points here include the castle, a theatre, fine old mansions and a local museum.

www.jumilla.org

➕ 14M (off map) ✉ 55km (34 miles) north of Murcia 🍴 Choice of restaurants and bars (€–€€€) 🚌 From Murcia

ℹ Plaza del Rollo 1 ☎ 968 78 02 37

Museo del Vino Juan Carcelén

✉ García Lorca 1 ☎ 679 78 82 51 for apppointment

Museo Municipal Jerónimo Molina

✉ Plaza de la Constitución 3 ☎ 968 78 07 40 🕓 May–Sep Tue–Sat 10:30–2, 5–8; Oct–Apr Tue–Sat 10:30–2, 5–8, Sun 11–1:30

EXPLORING

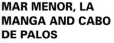

MAR MENOR, LA MANGA AND CABO DE PALOS

The Mar Menor, Murcia's holiday playground, was formed as sand and rocks gradually advanced outwards from two headlands, slowly transforming the original bay into a vast lagoon. The strip of land separating the lagoon from the Mediterranean is pierced by channels and is called La Manga, 'the sleeve'. This 24km-long (15-mile) ribbon of land, nowhere much more than a kilometre across, was totally undeveloped until the 1960s, a haunt of fishermen and birds. Today it's a solid strip of hotels, apartment blocks, shops, restaurants and bars, catering efficiently for a huge summer population of holiday-makers. The landward shore of the Mar saw some development in the 19th century when Spaniards from Murcia built spacious holiday homes at towns like Los Alcázares, San Javier and Santiago de la Ribera. These resorts are still popular with Spanish families.

Cabo de Palos, at the southern end of La Manga on the seaward side, is the closest to a traditional village, a jolly fishing and sailing centre, known for its lighthouse, Sunday market and good fish restaurants. The Mar Menor covers 170sq km (65sq miles) and is nowhere more than 7m (23ft) deep, making it a perfect watersports centre. Sailing, windsurfing and waterskiing are all available, and frequent excursion boats visit the lagoon's five islands. The seaward side of La Manga has some excellent diving areas and further south along the coast there are quiet coves and beaches (➤ 73).

www.marmenor.es

✚ 7A/B ✉ 55km (34 miles) east of Murcia ▮▮ Choice of restaurants and bars (€–€€€) 🚌 From Murcia 🚊 From Murcia 🚢 Excursions from Los Alcázares, Santiago de la Ribera and La Manga ❓ Hogueras de San Juan (24 Jun in San Pedro and San Javier)

ℹ️ Mar Menor: CN-332 Urbanización Oasis, Los Alcázares ☎ 968 17 13 61; Padre Juan s/n, Santiago de la Ribera ☎ 968 57 17 04; km 0 Las Amoladeras, La Manga del Mar Menor ☎ 968 14 61 36

MAZARRÓN

Lead, silver, iron and zinc were mined in Mazarrón from earliest historical times by Carthaginians, Romans and Arabs. The mines have been worked out for years, but some of the handsome buildings erected from mining profits remain. Defensive towers, built against Berber pirate attacks, survive, though the castle of Los Veléz is in ruins. The Torres de los Caballos, next to the convent of La Purísima, and the Torre Vieja de la Cumbre are worth a look, as is the beautiful *mudéjar* panelling in the church of San Andres. Today the town and its port thrive on tomatoes, fishing and tourists. The harbour doubles as a sailing and diving centre, while along the coast runs a string of deserted coves and beaches (➤ 73).

www.mazarron.es

✚ 4D ✉ 70km (43 miles) south of Murcia 🍴 Restaurants/bars (€–€€) 🚌 From Murcia ❓ Fallas de San José (12–20 Mar), Virgen del Carmen (16 Jul), Romería del Milagro de la Purísima (13–20 Nov) ℹ Plaza Toneleros ☎ 968 15 40 64

MULA

Situated by the Mula river, the town is packed with hidden delights and famed for its artisan traditions. Dominated by the 16th-century Castillo de los Veléz on the hill behind the town, the old quarter's narrow streets are scattered with fine buildings and churches, notably 16th-century Santo Domingo and San Miguel. The Museo del Cigarralejo is housed in a baroque mansion in the heart of town; its huge collection of Iberian art, excavated at a nearby necropolis, is one of Murcia's best. Within easy reach is the reservoir at La Cierva, and the little spa at Baños de Mula.

www.mulavirtual.es

✚ 6F (off map) ✉ 32km (20 miles) west of Murcia 🍴 Restaurants/bars (€–€€) 🚌 From Murcia ❓ Semana Santa (Mar/Apr) ℹ Convento de San Francisco, Calle Doña Elvira ☎ 968 66 15 01

SEGURA VALLEY (VALL DE SEGURA)

The Moors were the first to irrigate the Segura valley, making it incredibly fertile; they planted orange, almond and fruit orchards, and remained here until the 17th century. Still lovely, despite the inevitable development, the valley includes diverse landscapes and a scatter of interesting towns and villages. North of the spa town of Archena, citrus groves predominate, and the valley narrows through a gorge before widening out at the historic town of Ojós. Further on, Ricote, with its brightly coloured houses, is worth a stop before continuing towards Blanca. One of Spain's largest water wheels is at nearby Abarán; first installed by the Moors, several of these immense wooden machines still function. North of here, peach orchards stretch in all directions, before the hills start to close in once more and the valley finally reaches Calasparra, famous for its rice.

🚼 7F (off map) ✉ 30km (18.5 miles) northwest of Murcia 🍴 Choice of restaurants and bars (€–€€€)

ℹ Calasparra: Edificio Casa Granero 14 ☎ 968 74 53 25

SIERRA DE ESPUÑA

Best places to see, ➤ 54–55.

TOTANA

Quickly reached by motorway from Murcia, Totana lies on the edge of Murcia's splendid sierras, a good starting point for exploring the hill country. The town is mainly known for its pottery, made here since Moorish times. More than 20 potteries still produce an incredible range of ceramics, huge earthenware storage jars, pots and bowls. Some of these are still fired in the traditional Arab-style kiln, the *tosta*, where the pots stand on a perforated floor above the heat source. Workshops still produce the *cántara de Totana*, a traditional pitcher, probably first designed by the Romans. If you're shopping, head for the old pottery district in town, rather than the outlets aimed at the tourists along the main road.

www.totana.es

✚ 4F ✉ 35km (22 miles) south of Murcia ⑪ Choice of restaurants and bars (€–€€) 🚌 From Murcia

🛈 Calle General Aznar 12 ☎ 968 42 39 02

HOTELS

MURCIA
Arco de San Juan (€€€)
One of the city's great hotels, situated in Murcia's historic centre.
Tasteful and comfortable, hidden behind an 18th-century façade,
with a high level of friendly and professional service.
✉ Plaza Ceballos 10 ☎ 968 21 04 55; www.arcosanjuan.com

Hispano II (€€)
A traditional Murcian hotel in the historic centre near the cathedral
and main shops, with good service and comfortable rooms.
✉ Radio Murcia 3 ☎ 968 21 61 52; www.hotelhispano.net

ÁGUILAS
Al Sur (€€€)
Wonderfully situated on a promontory with great sea views, this
hotel has friendly proprietors and a laid-back atmosphere.
✉ Torre de Copa 24, Calabardina ☎ 968 41 94 66

Carlos III (€€)
A small hotel in the bustling centre of town, professionally and
courteously run, with comfortable rooms.
✉ Avenida Rey Carlos III 22 ☎ 968 41 16 50; www.hotelcarlosiii.com

CARAVACA DE LA CRUZ
Central (€€)
A good base for exploring the Segura valley, this small country
town hotel has comfortable rooms and friendly service.
✉ Gran Vía 18 ☎ 968 70 70 55

El Molino del Río (€€)
A converted 16th-century mill in a truly rural setting in the
undiscovered hinterland, high in the Argos valley system.
A mixture of self-catering and standard hotel-type accommodation
is offered here.
✉ Camoni Viejo de Archivel ☎ 968 43 33 81; www.molinodelrio.com

CARTAGENA
Best Western Alfonso XIII (€€€)
Cartagena's main central hotel, a classical building with spacious rooms and elegant architectural details. High level of service.
✉ Paseo Alfonso XIII 40 ☎ 968 52 00 00; www.hotelalfonsoxiii.com

FORTUNA
Balneario (€€)
A wonderful Edwardian spa hotel. The pool is fed by the hot springs and the hotel basement contains the treatment rooms.
✉ Balneario s/n ☎ 968 68 50 11; www.leana.es

LA MANGA DEL MAR MENOR
La Cavanna (€€€)
This vast hotel, overlooking the Mar Menor, has every conceivable facility and is a short walk from all the attractions.
✉ Plaza Cavanna s/n ☎ 968 56 36 00; www.izanhoteles.es

Dos Mares (€€)
A small, excellent value hotel right in the middle of the action.
✉ Plaza Bohemia s/n ☎ 968 14 30 46

Regency Hyatt Príncipe Felipe (€€€)
Murcia's only five-star hotel, with its own golf course and country-club atmosphere. Superb service and excellent restaurant.
✉ Los Belones ☎ 968 33 12 34; www.lamanga.regency.hyatt.com

MULA
Alcázar (€)
Ideal if you're touring the inland sierras; this quintessentially Spanish hotel has rather small rooms of great charm.
✉ Carretera Pliego s/n ☎ 968 66 21 05

PUERTO DE MAZARRÓN
Bahía (€€)
Right on the seafront. Simple décor and friendly staff.
✉ Playa de la Reya s/n ☎ 968 59 40 00; www.hotelbahia.com

SAN PEDRO DEL PINATAR
Balneario La Encarnación (€€)
A charming old-world spa hotel. Pretty tiled rooms and a warm welcome. (Open summer.)
✉ Condesa 8, Los Alcázares ☎ 968 57 50 04

RESTAURANTS

MURCIA
El Churra (€)
See page 58.

Mesón el Corral (€€)
See page 77.

✉ Plaza de San Juan s/n ☎ 968 22 06 75 🕐 Lunch and dinner. Closed Mon
✉ Calle San José 1 ☎ 968 22 17 26 🕐 Lunch and dinner. Closed Wed

Rincón del Pepe (€€€)
Stylish restaurant in a hotel of the same name, considered one of the best in Murcia. High-quality seafood and grilled meats.
✉ Apóstoles 34 ☎ 968 21 22 39 🕐 Lunch and dinner. Closed Sun pm

Rocío (€€)
Restaurant on the edge of the historic centre serving Murcian dishes as good as Rincón del Pepe (above) but at half the price.
✉ Batalla de las Flores s/n ☎ 968 24 29 30 🕐 Lunch and dinner. Closed Sun

CABO DE PALOS
Miramar (€€)
Big functional restaurant in a great position beside the sea, renowned for its fresh fish and lightest of frying.
✉ Paeso de la Barra 14 ☎ 968 56 30 33 🕐 Lunch and dinner. Closed Tue and Jan

El Mosqui (€€)
Housed in a building resembling an upturned boat and noted for its rice and fish; busy at weekends.

✉ Subida al Faro 50 ☎ 968 56 45 63 🕐 Lunch and dinner, weekends only in low season

CARAVACA DE LA CRUZ
Los Viñales (€)
Inland Murcian cooking. Excellent meat dishes, good vegetables, and cheese tart for pudding. Local wines only.
✉ Avenida Juan Carlos I 41 ☎ 968 70 84 58 🕐 Lunch and dinner. Closed Tue and for two weeks in Oct

CARTAGENA
Mare Nostrum (€€)
Low-key but elegant restaurant with the best sea views in town. Beautifully cooked local dishes, mainly fish and vegetables.
✉ Puerto Alfonso XII, Puerto Deportivo ☎ 968 52 21 31 🕐 Lunch and dinner

JUMILLA
Monasterio (€)
A large restaurant on the town outskirts. Functional with excellent food; a Spanish experience.
✉ Avenida de la Asunción 40 ☎ 968 78 20 92 🕐 Lunch and dinner. Closed Tue

Tasca Eulalia (€€)
See page 77.

LA MANGA DEL MAR MENOR
Amapola (€€€)
Even if you're not staying at the Hyatt Club you can eat at this elegant restaurant. Local ingredients with an international twist.
✉ Hyatt La Manga Club Resort, Los Belones ☎ 968 33 12 34 🕐 Lunch and dinner

LORCA
Cándido (€€)
Rustic old-fashioned restaurant. Try the classic local dish *trigo con conejo y caracoles* (wheat with rabbit and snails).
✉ Santo Domingo 13 ☎ 968 46 69 07 🕐 Lunch and dinner. Closed Sun eve

MULA
Venta La Magdalena (€)
First-rate upcountry cooking in simple surroundings, with plenty of locals eating. Excellent rabbit and rice dishes; house wine.

✉ Carretera Caravaca, Baños de Mula ☎ 968 66 05 68 🕐 Lunch and dinner. Closed Wed and 15 Jul–15 Aug

TOTANA
Venta de la Rata (€€)
Friendly restaurant specializing in every combination of rice, meat, fish and vegetables. Often busy at weekends.

✉ Carretera de la Santa Km 3 ☎ 968 42 09 09 🕐 Lunch and dinner. Closed Mon

SHOPPING

ARTS, CRAFTS AND GIFTS
Alfarería Bellón
A specialist ceramicist, making modern pots by using shapes, techniques and colours reminiscent of earlyIberian ware.

✉ Paseo de Ollerías 25, Totana ☎ 968 42 36 15

Centro Regional de Artesanía
Half-shop, half-exhibition, with the whole range of traditional Murcian handicrafts from all over the region.

✉ Francisco Rabal 8, Murcia ☎ 968 35 75 20 🕐 Mon–Sat 11–2, 5:30–8:30, Sun 12–2

El Poveo
A well-known outlet for one of Totana's major ceramic producers, with pots and other products beautifully made in interesting shapes and colours.

✉ Rambla s/n, Totana ☎ 968 42 19 52

Yelmo Antigüedades
One of the best antique shops in the Costa Blanca region but the prices are a bit on the high side.

✉ Sagasta 34 and 42, Cartagena ☎ 968 52 54 13

FOOD AND DRINK

Bodega Co-operativa San Isidro
Jumilla denominación de origen wines.
✉ Carretera Murcia 32, Jumilla ☎ 968 78 07 00

Confitería Carlos
A mecca for the sweet-toothed with cakes, pastries and traditional sweetmeats that are beautiful to look at and delicious to eat.
✉ Calle Jaime I 7–Bajo, Murcia ☎ 968 23 30 20

Fonda Negra
Old-established shop with a large range of high-quality Murcian foodstuffs.
✉ González Adalid 1, Murcia ☎ 968 21 15 63

ENTERTAINMENT

BARS AND NIGHTCLUBS

Discoteca The Night Club
Really starts to hum after 1am when most people arrive.
✉ Puerta Nueva, Murcia ☎ None ⏰ Daily 11:30pm–6am, Thu–Sat

Zeppelin
One of the liveliest of the disco bars along La Manga's main boulevard, with the action starting late and continuing often until after dawn.
✉ Gran Via de la Manga, La Manga ☎ None ⏰ Daily 11pm–6am

CASINOS

Casino Cartagena
✉ Mayor 15, Cartagena ☎ 968 52 55 77 ⏰ Daily 10–2, 5–11

Casino del Mar Menor
✉ Gran Via La Manga s/n, La Manga ☎ 968 14 06 04 ⏰ Sun–Thu 9pm–4am, Fri, Sat 9pm–5am

Gran Casino Murcia
✉ Apóstoles 34, Murcia ☎ 968 21 23 08 ⏰ Daily 6pm–4am

THEATRE
Teatro Romea
Full programme of Spanish theatre and music.

✉ Plaza Julián Romea 7, Murcia ☎ 968 35 53 90; www.teatroromea.org

SPORT

GOLF
Club de Golf Torre Pacheco

✉ Torre Pacheco, La Manga ☎ 968 58 51 11; www.golftorrepacheco.com

La Manga Club

✉ Los Belones, La Manga ☎ 968 17 50 00; www.lamangaclub.com

HORSE-RIDING
El Puntal

✉ La Manga Club Hyatt Complex, Los Belones, La Manga ☎ 968 13 73 05

Peque Park

✉ La Manga del Mar Menor, La Manga ☎ 908 86 25 69

SAILING
Club Náutico Islas Menores

✉ Paseo Marítimo s/n, Murcia ☎ 968 13 33 44

Club Náutico Mazarrón

✉ Calle Paseo de la Sal s/n, Mazarrón ☎ 609 36 02 60

Surf-Playa

✉ La Manga del Mar Menor, La Manga ☎ 968 14 00 20

SCUBA DIVING
Islas Hormigas Club

✉ Paseo de la Barra 15 ☎ 968 14 55 30

Zoea Mazarrón

✉ Plaza del Mar 20, Mazarrón ☎ 968 15 40 06

Sight Locator Index

This index relates to the maps on the covers. We have given map references to the main sights of interest in the book. Grid references in italics indicate sights featured on the town plans. Some sights within towns may not be plotted on the maps.

187

Index

Acknowledgements

The Automobile Association would like to thank the following photographers and companies for their assistance in the preparation of this book.

Abbreviations for the picture credits are as follows – (t) top; (b) bottom; (c) centre; (l) left; (r) right; (AA) AA World Travel Library

4l Castle ramparts of Jativa, AA/M Chaplow; **4c** Villajoyosa, AA/M Chaplow; **4r** Gardens of Huerto del Cura, Elche, AA/M Chaplow; **5l** Castillo de Santa Barbara, Alicante, AA/M Chaplow; **5c** Street scene, Alicante, AA/M Chaplow; **6/7** Castle ramparts of Jativa, AA/M Chaplow; **8/9** Coastal scene, Costa Blanca, AA/M Chaplow; **10/11t** Beach, Javea, AA/J Edmanson; **10bl** La Virgen de la Consuelo, Altea, AA/M Chaplow; **11cl** Alicante, AA/M Chaplow; **11bl** Colourful house, Alicante, AA/M Chaplow; **12bl** Rice and seafood dish, AA/M Chaplow; **12/13t** Stall, Castellon de la Plana, AA/J Edmanson; **12/13b** Oranges, AA/P Baker; **13cr** Papas Arugadas (potato dish), AA/J Tims; **13br** Tapas bar, Murcia, AA/J Edmanson; **14/15t** Restaurant, AA/M Chaplow; **14b** Tapas, AA/M Chaplow; **15tr** Wine bottle, AA/M Chaplow; **15c** Orange grove, Benidorm, AA/M Chaplow; **15bl** Mercado central, Alicante, AA/M Chaplow; **15br** Café, Traperia, Murcia, AA/M Chaplow; **16c** Playa de Levante, Benidorm, AA/M Chaplow; **16bl** Costa Blanca Express, AA/M Chaplow; **17t** Playa Levante, Calpe, AA/J Edmanson; **17b** Explanada de Espana, Alicante, AA/J Edmanson; **18/19t** Wine, AA/S McBride; **18cr** Flamenco, AA/M Jourdan; **18bl** Denia, AA/M Chaplow; **19b** Flower stall, AA/M Chaplow; **20/21** Villajoyosa, AA/M Chaplow; **24** Violinists, Digital Vision; **25b** Explanada de Espana, Alicante, AA/M Chaplow; **27** Aeroplane, Digital Vision; **28/29** Car travelling, AA/M Chaplow; **31** Payphone, AA/M Chaplow; **34/35** Gardens of Huerto del Cura, AA/M Chaplow; **36bl** Calblanque, AA/M Chaplow; **37t** Calblanque, AA/M Chaplow; **38bl** Castillo de Santa Barbara, AA/M Chaplow; **38/39** Castillo de Santa Barbara, AA/M Chaplow; **39tr** Detail, Castillo de Santa Barbara, AA/M Chaplow; **40bl** Berries, Gallinera Valley, AA/M Chaplow; **41t** Gallinera Valley, AA/M Chaplow; **41br** Church, Gallinera Valley, AA/M Chaplow; **42** Guadalest Valley, AA/M Chaplow; **43** Castle, Guadalest, AA/J Edmanson; **44-45** Huerto del Cura, AA/M Chaplow; **46cr** Montgo Natural Park, AA/M Chaplow; **46b** Montgo, AA/M Chaplow; **47t** Disused windmills, Cabo San Antonio, AA/M Chaplow; **49tr** Costa Blanca coast, AA/M Chaplow; **49b** Penon de Ifach, Calpe, AA/M Chaplow; **51** Church of San Feliu, Jativa, Stuart Black/The Travel Library; **52cl** Cathedral, Murcia, AA/J Edmanson; **52/53b** Cathedral, Murcia, AA/J Edmanson; **53t** Cathedral, Murcia, AA/M Chaplow; **53br** Cathedral, Murcia, AA/M Chaplow; **55** Sierra de Espuna, AA/M Chaplow; **56/57** Castillo de Santa Barbara, Alicante, AA/M Chaplow; **59** Stained-glass, restaurant Casa Enrique, Elche, AA/M Chaplow; **60/61** Benidorm, AA/M Chaplow; **62/63** Golf, AA/M Chaplow; **64b** Giraffe, Safari Park, Sierra de Aitana, AA/M Chaplow; **65t** Benimantell, AA/J Edmanson; **66/67** Market, AA/M Chaplow; **68/69** Cloisters of Alicante's 17th-century Church of San Nicolás de Bari, AA/M Chaplow; **71t** Beach, Cala Bassa, AA/J Tims; **71c** Goat, Sierra de Aitana Safari Park, AA/M Chaplow; **72/73** Beach, Gandia, AA/J Edmanson; **74b** Museo Salzillo, AA/M Chaplow; **76** Tapas, AA/M Chaplow; **78/79** Castle, Sax, AA/M Chaplow; **80/81** Street scene, Alicante, AA/M Chaplow; **83** View from Castello Santa Barbara to Alicante, AA/M Chaplow; **85** Clock tower of the Ayuntamiento, Alicante, AA/M Chaplow; **86-87** San Nicolas de Bari, AA/M Chaplow; **88-89** Explanada de Espana, Alicante, AA/M Chaplow; **90-91** Cathedral, Orihuela, AA/M Chaplow; **92** Colegio de Santo Domingo, AA/M Chaplow; **95** Cuevas de Canalobre, Busot, AA/M Chaplow; **96t** Fortress, Elche, AA/J Edmanson; **97b** Palms, Elche, AA/J Edmanson; **98-99** Guardamar del Segura, AA/M Chaplow; **100t** Vineyards, Monovar, AA/M Chaplow; **100c** Vineyards, Monovar, AA/M Chaplow; **101** La Mola Tower, Novelda, AA/M Chaplow; **102tl** Fisherman, Santa Pola, AA/M Chaplow; **103b** Castle, Sax, AA/M Chaplow; **105** Torrevieja, AA/M Chaplow; **106tl** La Atalaya watchtower, Villena, AA/M Chaplow; **119** Street scene, Altea, AA/M Chaplow; **120/121** Benidorm, AA/J Edmanson; **121t** Poolside, Benidorm, AA/M Chaplow; **122** San Jaime Church, Benidorm, AA/M Chaplow; **123t** L'Aiguera Park, AA/M Chaplow; **124/125c** Mirador, overlooking Benidorm, AA/M Chaplow; **124bl** Geraniums, Placa de la Senora, AA/J Edmanson; **125r** Benidorm, AA/J Edmanson; **126bl** El Castillo, Jativa, AA/M Chaplow; **127** Jativa, AA/M Chaplow; **128tl** Hospital Real, AA/M Chaplow; **128/129** Statue of Jativa-born painter Jose de Ribera, AA/M Chaplow; **129br** Virgin and Child carving, Hospital Real, AA/M Chaplow; **130-131** Alcoy, AA/M Chaplow; **132** Altea, AA/M Chaplow; **133t** La Virgen de la Consuelo, Altea, AA/M Chaplow; **134/135** View from Cabo de San Martin of Isla de Portitxol, AA/M Chaplow; **136bl** Tower at Cocentaina, AA/M Chaplow; **137** Palau Comtal, Cocentaina, AA/M Chaplow; **138t** Denia, AA/M Chaplow; **139t** Denia, AA/M Chaplow; **139b** Fonts de L'Algar, AA/M Chaplow; **140** Beach, Gandia, AA/J Edmanson; **141** Gorgos Valley, AA/M Chaplow; **142/143c** Almond trees, AA/M Chaplow; **142b** Guadalest Valley, AA/M Chaplow; **143tr** Plaza de la Iglesia, Javea, AA/M Chaplow; **144bl** Castle walls, Moraira, AA/M Chaplow; **144/145** Moraira, AA/M Chaplow; **145tr** Oliva, AA/J Edmanson; **146bl** Casa de la Villa, Pego, AA/M Chaplow; **146/147** Fonts de L'Algar, AA/M Chaplow; **147br** Pego, AA/M Chaplow; **148cl** Sierra d'Aitana, AA/M Chaplow; **149t** Sierra d'Aitana, AA/S Watkins; **149b** Sierra de Aitana, AA/M Chaplow; **150-151** Villajoyosa, AA/M Chaplow; **161** Castillo de los Velez, Mula, AA/M Chaplow; **162-163** Casino, Murcia, AA/M Chaplow; **165b** Cathedral, Murcia, AA/J Edmanson; **166** Glorieta Espana, Murcia, AA/M Chaplow; **167** Plaza Santo Domingo, Murcia, AA/M Chaplow; **168bl** Aguilas, AA/M Chaplow; **168/169** Aguilas, AA/M Chaplow; **169tr** Aguilas, AA/J Edmanson; **170-171** Cartagena, AA/M Chaplow; **172t** Fortuna, AA/M Chaplow; **173b** Town hall, Jumilla, Bildarchiv Monheim GmbH/Alamy; **174-175** Mar Menor, AA/M Chaplow; **177** Santo Domingo church, Mula, AA/M Chaplow; **178/179** Segura Valley, AA/M Chaplow.

Every effort has been made to trace the copyright holders, and we apologise in advance for any accidental errors. We would be happy to apply the corrections in the following edition of this publication.